Also by Yvonne F. Conte

Serious Laughter—Live a Happier,
Healthier, More Productive Life

Remarkable Women of Faith—Testimonies
from America's Women of Faith

Bits of Joy—150 Ideas That Will Make You Jump for Joy

Frankie Wonders—A Child's Look at September 11, 2001

Make a BIG Deal—
How to Be a Motivational Speaker and Best Selling Author

Cry, Laugh, Cook!—A Collection of Essays,
Conversations, and Conte Family Recipes

One
Word

Stories of
Influence,
Enlightenment,
and Hope

Yvonne F. Conte
and Friends

Amsterdam Berwick
PUBLISHING

One Word, Stories of Influence, Enlightenment, and Hope

Published by Amsterdam Berwick Publishing

Editing, design, and typesetting by Richard Groff, TypeSmith

For information address:
Amsterdam Berwick Publishing
Attn: Permissions Coordinator
109 Big Bend Way
Warners, NY 13164

Special Day of Joy, Incorporated, Edition

Printed in the United States of America

2   4   6   8   10   9   7   5   3   1

First Edition

Library of Congress Cataloging-in Publication Data
Conte, Yvonne F., 1951–
One word: stories of influence, enlightenment, and hope /
Yvonne F. Conte—Amsterdam Berwick Publishing.
        p.   cm.
1. Self-realization.   2. American wit and humor.   1. Title.

ISBN 978-0-9665336-9-9

Publisher's Note

All monies earned by the author from sales of
this book in the United States will go to the
women's ministry, Day of Joy, Incorporated.

All monies earned by the author from sales of this book in Canada
will go to the women's ministry, Day of Joy, Incorporated.

All monies earned by the author from sales of this
book outside the United States and Canada will go to
the women's ministry, Day of Joy, Incorporated.

All contributors retain the rights to their stories as they appear in
One Word. None of the contributors have been paid. Each has shared
freely so that all profits go to the Day of Joy Ministry. As this book
goes to press, approximately $28,000 has been given to eight charities
who help women to build stronger families, stronger communities,
and stronger church families. Together we can change lives.

There are many ways to support this ministry—certainly praying
for women worldwide who are struggling, telling others about the
Day of Joy ministry and the work that we do, and your monetary
gifts support Day of Joy so that we can continue to help women
become better women.

To make a gift donation or to receive materials about Day of Joy
send us your name, address, city, state, postal code, country, and
email address and send it to:

Day of Joy, Incorporated
1624 Pine Valley Dr. 7–302
Fort Myers, FL 33907
www.dayofjoy.org

Acknowledgments

MANY PEOPLE HAVE IMPACTED my life and my heart and have helped me grow, learn, and go in the direction of my dreams. Many of them have shared their personal stories here, revealing those who have influenced and encouraged them. Without their kindness and generosity we wouldn't have anything to print! I thank all for their eagerness to share their story; however, I also thank you for purchasing this book and supporting the Day of Joy ministry. Many of you have given generously, donated time and talents, sponsored our conferences, been vendors, and purchased tickets to our events. You are appreciated. Most important, I thank our volunteers who work tirelessly before, during, and after our conferences, ensuring that all aspects of the day are perfect. Above all, I thank the Holy Spirit for always showing up and guiding our way. For this I thank you deeply.

Central New York Leadership

Shannon Beaulieu	Katie Lemos Brown
Suzanne Cucola	Michelle Morin Wilkinson
Patricia Duffy	Rachel Mosher
Cindy Ferguson	Susan Sweeney
Theresa Harris	Shelly Thompson-Liedka
Cheri Lauffer	

Florida Leadership

Pam Elcik	Melanie Nicholl
Joanna JoJo Koenig	Patti Marks

Tennessee Leadership

Tonja Benard	Barbara Holbrook
Denise Sherriff	

Table of Contents

This book is dedicated to:

GOD THE FATHER
*for changing my life with His Word
and for His constant love*

ANGELA TORSELLA CONTE
*who ignited my passion for reading, writing,
an elegantly set table, and beautiful music*

FRANK WILLIAM CONTE
*who taught me that the greatest gift to give
is the gift of laughter
and that life was to be savored
and enjoyed with gusto!*

PROVERBS 25:11
Like apples of gold in settings of silver
is a word spoken at the right time.

Introduction

AT DAY OF JOY, we contact local businesses to help provide products we need for our conferences. One morning I was on the lookout for a company that may be able to provide fruit for our breakfast and breaks. I remembered that when I was a young child my dad had a friend in the produce business. His name was Frank Insera and he owned Syracuse Banana Company. I laughed at myself. How did I remember that random fact when I can't even remember where I put my keys?

I quickly googled Syracuse Banana Company and found it was still in business and still located in the same spot. My father had been gone nearly twenty years and the chance that anyone who had worked there that long ago would still be there was slim. I walked in and asked the lady at the desk if Frank Insera still owed the company. She said that he had passed away many years ago but that his son Steve was now running the company. "Well," I said, "he may not remember me, but my dad and his dad were great friends. Any chance he would speak to me for a few minutes? Just tell him Frank Conte's daughter Yvonne is here." She picked up the phone and said, "I have an Yvonne Conte here to see you." She put down the phone and said. "He'll be right out."

Within seconds Steve ran up to me and gave me a big bear hug, "Yvonne! What a nice surprise! How in the world are you?" Truth be told, I didn't remember him. However, somehow, he remembered me and ushered me into his office. We had a great talk about families and business and life in general. Then he asked me what had brought me to his door. I told him all about the Day of Joy and explained that I was looking for a donation for the conference. He asked how many women generally attend. I told him we were expecting 800. I said I'd appreciate any amount of bananas or apples he would be willing to offer. His next words will stay with me forever; he said, "For Frank Conte, I'll give you all the bananas and apples you want!" Imagine that! He was generous to me, simply because my father had left an impression on him. Twenty years after my father's death, a young boy remembered the kind of man he was, and because of that was generous to me.

When someone has lived on this earth, and twenty years after that person's death your life is impacted by the type of person they were, you get a sense that their positive influence will continue for generations to come.

Many of the principles my father used to lead, to guide, and to inspire others, are the same ones I try to utilize in every area of my life.

My father taught me many things, but one thing he said to me will stay with me forever. He said, "Whatever you choose to do with your life, make sure you are thinking about how it affects the lives of others. If you do that, you will always feel joy in the work that you do." He was right. In my work as a motivational speaker and as a volunteer director of Day of Joy, I work hard to build up the lives of others, to encourage and inspire them to do and be better. I receive so much joy in the process.

His influence and how it formed the person I am today made me wonder if others have had this same type of person in their lives and what it would mean to collect their stories in a book. As I began to collect these stories I realized that we all have a responsibility to be aware of how we influence others.

There is an incredible amount of wisdom between the covers of this book. Each story is a bit different. All of them are full of inspiration, encouragement, and the importance of those that came before us. Words are powerful. A few simple words can change a person's life forever. Open the pages of this book and through the stories here you will find encouragement and hope and, in some cases, you will see how *One Word* can have a lifetime impact.

Our first essay is written by nationally known comedian Sky Sands. He tells us how he learned that the only person he had to change and get to like him . . . was himself.

The greatness of
a man is not in
how much wealth
he acquires, but
in his integrity
and his ability to
affect those around
him positively.

—Bob Marley

Sky Sands

Sky Sands has been described as a Comedian, Magician, Actor, Writer, Entertainer, Corporate EnterTrainer, and refers to himself as a Possibilitarian. "Anything is possible." Sky has been a featured act on several cruise lines, has performed in Las Vegas and Atlantic City, playing such places as the Tropicana Hotel and Resort, the MGM Grand, the Flamingo, and Las Vegas Hilton resorts. He has appeared on Cinemax, Showtime, VH-I, and MSNBC. He appears nationally as well as internationally, having performed in Italy, Germany, Austria, Hungry, Mexico and Aruba. Sky has won several awards for his work in broadcasting, including three Telly Awards for writing and acting in the United Way's "Volunteer Connection" campaign. He can now be seen on television on his own show called "Origami with Sky Sands," where he can be found teaching the ancient art of origami in a very amusing way on several stations across the country. Sky volunteers much of his time to benefit area charities, and most recently was awarded the Outstanding Service Award for his involvement with Public Radio's "Reach Out Radio" program. When asked why he does what he's been doing for so many years, Sky replied, "I love what I do, and I know I'm blessed to be able to share it with others." Sky lives in Rochester, NY, with his wife Andréa and dog Wilson.

Wisdom Around the Campfire

Sky Sands

As soon as John asked me to meet him that night at the fire circle, I started getting nervous. We were cleaning the tables after lunch, and John walked over to me. John was the cook at the summer camp where I worked. I was seventeen years old, a first-time junior counselor, filled with determination, enthusiasm, and a pretty strong appearing (but pretty shaky sense) of self-confidence. John said that he had something that he wanted to share with me, and that I might find it to be a real eye opener. He told me to meet him at the fire circle after lights-out, once the kids had turned in for the night.

John was a nice guy and we had joked around a bit from time to time, but I was wary of John, a Born Again Christian. To me, someone who was "born again" was similar to a Jehovah's Witness at my doorstep. I never saw the encounter as an exchange of dialogue or ideas but as the person that would be on the receiving end of a lecture, or even a "sales pitch" at that. That assumption came from a few past experiences, but mostly what I had heard from other people.

The camp was sponsored by the Jewish Community Center, and although it was regarded as multidenominational, it held Friday-night sabbath services and kept a kosher kitchen. So, although it was open to anyone, it was the Jewish religion that predominated the spiritual side of the camp.

I knew that John mostly kept his religion to himself, but once he said he wanted to talk to me—alone—I didn't know what to expect. Actually, I did. I expected him to start talking to me about accepting Jesus Christ as my savior, and since it would just be the two of us, I was afraid of being cornered and being put on the spot. I did not want to become Born Again. Actually, I didn't know what I wanted to be. If you were to ask me back then if I was a Jew, I would have answered "Well . . . I'm Jew*ish*. I was raised Jewish, but at an early age I was looking into and learning about other religions, cultures, and beliefs, preferring to avoid the ones based largely on guilt. (Jews and Catholics are very similar in that area.)

With the kids in their bunks and my co-counselor on watch, I made my way to the fire circle. As I approached, I saw that John had just finished lighting a fire he'd put together. This wasn't going to be a quick chat. Putting a fire together was a commitment. Someone would have to be there for a couple of hours. There was always a chance others would stop by, but for now it was just the two of us. He saw me approach, so there was no way I could get out of this. I was scrambling to think of ways to let him know I wasn't interested. With a deep breath, I walked over to the circle. John left the blazing fire and joined me on the bench where I was sitting.

"Thanks for meeting with me tonight." he said. "Comfortable?"

"Sure." In truth, I was nervous about what he was going to say, and how I was going to get out of this.

A minute of silence—both of us looking into the fire.

He turned toward me and said, "First off, I'm going to need you to empty your cup."

"What cup?"

"Good question. Allow me to answer with this little story," and turning back to the fire, he said, "There was once a young man who wanted to become wiser and learn all that there was to learn from the wisest man in his village. He went to the man one day and said 'I'm ready, teacher. I want to learn all there is to learn so I can become a better person and understand the world around me. I'm ready. I know I'm ready, so please, if you would, teach me what you know. Would you? I'm ready, and you can start any time. I know what I want to learn, and I know what I need to learn, and I'm ready for you to teach me.' "

"The old man turned and picked up a tea cup and handed it to the would-be student. He then picked up a tea kettle and began pouring tea into the cup. The tea cup filled, nearing the top.

" 'Thank you,' said the young man, but the older man continued to pour the tea, which soon began to run over the top of the cup.

" 'Stop! It's full!' he cried, but the old man continued to pour tea from the teapot, and it overflowed the cup and spilled onto the floor below.

" 'Stop! Stop pouring! The cup is full! It can't hold anymore!'

"And with that the old man stopped pouring and said, 'That's right, it can hold no more. Just like this cup, you must empty your own vessel before it can take in anything more that is new.' "

John stopped talking and we both just sat there in silence. I was about to ask him what the story meant, but for some reason I remained silent.

After a few minutes John turned to me and simply asked, "Well?"

I knew what he was asking. "It's empty." I said.

He smiled.

He said, "Sky, I know you are new at being a counselor, and it's obvious that you're excited about it. It's also obvious to those on the the staff that you are trying very hard to get the kids to like you, and what you do—your magic tricks, the juggling, the craziness and wackiness that makes you *you*. You are trying so hard. The thing is, you could be trying *too* hard. I know it's fun when some of these kids emulate what you do, but this is a summer camp. Camp Seneca Lake, not Camp Sky. Not all of your kids are going to marvel at or be into the things you do. When you get them excited about what you do, that's great. Let 'em enjoy it. But you don't have to force-feed them. That's what I've picked up from watching you with the kids."

I was about to get defensive and reply to what he said, but I waited a second too long and he continued.

"Kids—they're like . . . clay. They're soft and pliable. You can mold them and shape them. They can become wonderful "pieces of art," each one unique. But once we start getting older, the clay begins to harden, and it becomes harder to change the shape of what has been created, and when the clay turns to stone—which it often does with many people—you have to chip away, to change the shape, or introduce new ideas before they become set in their ways. These kids are still "clay." Take your time with them. Know that what you say and do will have some effect on how they take shape. Are you following me so far?"

"I think so," I answered.

"Good. And finally, it's like the story of Johnny Appleseed; how he walked through the countryside and scattered apple seeds as he went. In some places seeds would take root and grow into fruit-bearing trees. These kids are kind of like the apple seeds. You come in contact with them. You have something to share with them. Some are going to love what you have to share with them and run with it, and others, they won't seem to care. Not every seed grows. You can't ignore those who don't seem to be taking root. Nurture the seeds that begin to grow and know that what you have to share with them may stay with them for many years and, in turn, they may share what they received from you with others."

This was my first introduction to what would take me decades to learn:

- Keep an open mind. You can't learn what you think you already know. "The cup has to be emptied" before anything new can be put into it.
- Take your time and appreciate the beauty of children. Their potential is boundless, and how they take shape, what influences their "molding", differs with each and every child. Hard clay can still be reshaped; it just needs more time and patience.
- You can't please everyone. Not everyone is going to appreciate what you have to share. That's okay. It's not about you. It's about others. It's about the positive, the good that you put out there, and that is taken in by others. Taken and appreciated.

We both sat there, staring at the fire.

John broke the silence. "Are you okay?"

I nodded. "Yeah, I think I am."

"This wasn't what you thought I wanted to talk to you about, was it?"

"Honestly . . . no."

"What did you think?" He turned and faced me. "That I was going to try to convert you?"

"Something like that."

He nodded and smiled. I remember his face, lit up be the campfire as he smiled and said, "Now you know. You have to empty your cup."

I went to our meeting, expecting one thing, with half of a mental wall built up, ready and on guard to defend myself against what he might say. But I walked away from it loving the idea that I didn't have to know everything or influence every person I met. Sometimes, our teachers find us.

It was many years later that I came to realize that that was the first lesson in learning that the only person I had to change and get to like me—was *me*.

I'm still a work in progress.

Tea, anyone?

In every walk with nature one receives far more than he seeks.

—JOHN MUIR

Aubry Ludington Panek

Aubry Ludington Panek is President and Boss Lady at Witty Wicks Candle Shop, 69 Main Street, Camillus, NY. She is an accomplished actor and vocalist and is mom to three great boys and wife to husband Todd. Visit www.wittywicks.com.

A Word About Teachers

Aubry Ludington Panek

In fourth grade I sat next to a kid who shoved a dime so far up his nose it got stuck and started to bleed profusely all over his desk. When my teacher asked "What happened Paul?" He just looked at her and said "Um, shoved a dime up my nose," as if shoving a dime up his nose was normal.

At least once a year some kid would get sick all over the classroom and before the janitor could get there with the sawdust, my teacher would have to keep everyone out of the mess and somehow get us to focus on anything besides the smell in the room.

Teachers deal with children who come from situations that are less than perfect. Children from single-parent households, low-income families, abuse, neglect, children with special needs—the list is endless.

It's important to understand that something you might say one day could change the direction of a child's life. That's how important and influential a teacher can be to a child.

Music was a huge part of my family. My father was a musician, my maternal grandmother was a professional vocalist, and my younger brother is a musical genius. Everywhere we went my brother would bring along his guitar. At every family gathering or party, he was always asked to sing and play. I remember that I wanted nothing more than to be able to sing, but no one ever asked me. I felt sometimes as if I wasn't good enough. Once my brother started to sing, I felt invisible.

My first opportunity to prove myself was in middle school. I auditioned for the school musical. I didn't have the nerve to try out for a role, but I was happy to be able to sing in the choir. In eighth grade my brother tried out for a role and sibling rivalry set in. I couldn't bare the thought of my little brother having a leading role and leaving me behind in the chorus. If he was trying out for a role, I had to at least give it a shot. The day came and my bother got up to sing. The place went wild. Everybody clapped. He was a shoe-in for the lead. My turn came. I got up and sang my song. Afterward, my teacher said, "Oh, honey, you should never sing alone. You should just sing in the chorus."

I was embarrassed and wished I hadn't even tried out in the first place. Interestingly enough, I did end up with a big part in the play and I even had a solo. But it wasn't my talent that got me the role; it was my height. I was the tallest kid in the class and the only one who could play the principal of the school.

When it came time for my solo, my teacher made me speak it. I had so looked forward to my opportunity to sing and she made me speak it. I was heartbroken. My dreams of stardom were crushed on that stage. For years I heard her voice in my head reinforcing all of my adolescent insecurities. "I'm not good enough; I can't sing; I have no talent." In my first year of high school I made it into the chorus of the school musical. I was so excited. I loved everything about the stage and was proud to have made it into the chorus. The following year I got up the nerve to audition for a part in the fall play. I was so scared I made my mother come with me to the audition. When we walked in I overheard someone say we had to read a monologue. I freaked out and said, "Never mind, Mom. Let's go."

As we left the auditorium the theater director, Mr. Minardi, walked up to us and said, "Hi, Aubry! Hi Yvonne! Glad you're here," and kept walking past us.

I was stunned that he actually knew my name and my mother's. I was just a girl in the chorus and he remembered me. I turned around and followed him into the theater. I auditioned. I was in that play and every single musical and play for the rest of my high school career. After high school I moved to New York City where I spent ten years as a professional actor/singer. I toured all over the United States and internationally.

I had been an average student in high school. I wasn't into sports; I wasn't a cheerleader; I wasn't on student council. I was simply a good kid with average grades. Until the tenth grade, I felt invisible. If Mr. Minardi had just walked by me that day without saying hello— without knowing my name—I would have simply left the theater and I wouldn't be the woman I am today. The entire path of my life might have changed. Teachers have that power every day in the work they do with children. Just one word could change their path. A simple hello. It's an awesome responsibility.

Tom Minardi was a constant mentor, not just to me, but for so many other kids that went through my high school. Twenty-seven years have past but I still hear his words of encouragement in my head: "You can do this, Aubry. You have talent. Your life has value."

Twenty-seven years from now, what will your students remember about you? Maybe one word you say—one action you take—could change the direction and path of a child's life without your even realizing it. That is how important teachers are and how important the work that they do is.

I know many of you have much more training and experience in child development than I do. I'm not a social worker. I'm not a psychologist. I have no formal training in child development. I'm just a mom who is doing the best I can because it's the most important job I've ever had. Being a parent is the hardest job I've ever done. Mostly it's hard because I find myself struggling some days to just keep my head above water; sleepless nights, temper tantrums, figuring out how to make discipline effective, and so many other struggles. Then there's the constant wondering, Am I doing this right? Did I pick the right nursery school? Am I giving good advice about bullies? Did I take away the pacifier too soon? Are they on the computer too much?

There are similar concerns with your pupils, and on any given day you have possibly two hundred kids you could influence. More than four million babies are born in the United States each year; sweet babies born into a world they know nothing about. I wonder what contributions they will make and how they might change this world. What will they become? How will they be influenced? Whose actions will motivate them, and whose beliefs will shape their minds?

The massive responsibility we have as adults is almost overwhelming. Every single thing we do—each word we utter and every action we take—will be observed by the children in our lives and they will be affected by it. That makes me want to be a better person *immediately*. Sociologists tell us that even the most introverted person will influence 10,000 people in his or her lifetime! Some will be a good influence and others . . . not so much.

Tomorrow your classrooms will be filled with the leaders of our future. The Pauls with dimes up their noses, the sick kids, the insecure kids, the troublemakers, the brownnosers, and the invisible kids. What kind of influence will you be on their lives? Just remember that I am who I am today because one teacher remembered my name.

William Arthur Ward, the author of many inspirational maxims, said, "Flatter me, and I may not believe you. Criticize me, and I may not like you. Ignore me, and I may not forgive you. Encourage me, and I will not forget you."

A good teacher can inspire hope,
ignite the imagination,
and instill a love of learning.
—BRAD HEN

Good teachers know how to bring out the best in students.

—CHARLES KURALT

Kristin Onderdonk

Kristin Onderdonk is the owner and CEO of Enjoy Chi, a wellness company she began more than four years ago, transitioning from a CPA in public accounting into coaching and consulting. She is certified in Applied Functional Science as a movement coach, a certified Tai Chi instructor, a Reiki Master, as well as a top leader and consultant for Neal's Yard Remedies, certified organic health and beauty products. Kristin's mission at Enjoy Chi is to share proven mind-body-spirit self-care initiatives for all people to incorporate into their lives. Kristin has led and assisted movement classes, conditioning, as well as sport-specific injury preventative and running programming at several local facilities. She has trained with and worked directly alongside various health industry experts, and is recognized as an expert in moving meditation and in providing wellness to her clients. She has worked with individuals all across the globe. Enjoy Chi is a Certified New York State Women-Owned Business. Visit www.enjoychi.com.

Perfect Is an Illusion; Bring Tissues Wherever You Go!

Kristin Onderdonk

In 2005 I remarried and went from one child to three children and a husband who traveled overnight for work. Determined to be the perfect mom, step-mom, CPA, and wife, I aimed to please everyone. I was totally overwhelmed. This was not how perfect looked or felt. Enough was enough! I knew something was about to blow.

It was Friday morning. I couldn't wait for my husband to get home from his business trip. For the fifth straight day I roused and fed two teens and a kindergartener, remembered their lunches, and raced to catch the bus. I was stressed.

It was 7:20 A.M., picture day at school, and we were just a block from the house when my kindergartener screamed, "It's up my nose!"

"What!?" I shouted back as I pulled the car over. Somehow she had snuffed a Tic Tac right up her left nostril. Out of sheer frustration, desperate to save our perfect morning, I admonished her for having done such a thing, and tried stretching her nostril open in search of the missing Tic Tac.

"My nose is on fire!" she yelled.

I called my husband in Philly and he suggested we go to urgent care. I called our pediatrician and got the answering service.

"What's the reason for your call this morning?" I was asked.

"My five-year-old sniffed a Tic Tac up her nose."

I was told that a nurse would get back to me in twenty or thirty minutes, so I headed for the nearest urgent care.

On the way, a nurse from my pediatrician's office called. I said I was on my way to an urgent care. "Turn around!" she said. "Don't go to urgent care. Go to the ER."

"Seriously?" I asked.

"Yes. Urgent care is inept at foreign objects," she went on, most likely thinking the same thing about me, so I didn't question further.

Nurse Know-It-All stayed on the line to provide me turn-by-turn directions, and faxed the ER: "Mom is on her way with daughter and a Tic Tac."

"It's okay," she assured me, and told me about how her son once put a Cocoa Puff up his nose and almost aspirated it.

That's reassuring, I thought.

She added, "My daughter broke a crayon off in her ear once and almost went deaf."

"You're on speakerphone," I warned her.

"Stay calm, ma'am," she said. "I need you to watch her color."

"But I'm driving," I said. "She's quiet now."

It was rush hour and it was pouring rain. Just breathe! I told myself. We arrived at the ER and I raced through security, shouting, "WE HAVE AN EMERGENCY!"

The triage nurse started asking me questions. Height, weight, would I like a tissue? Nose dripping, my daughter took the tissue and blew once, twice, three times, and out popped the partly melted, minty Tic-Tac.

The nurse looked up at me and with a sly smile, said, "Do you want to forget you were ever here?"

Out the revolving doors, past the security guard, to our car we fled. "Yup! Another miracle in the books!?" I replied.

I headed to Catholic kindergarten in stunned silence. So much for perfect attendance, I thought. The nuns will love this tardy excuse. My daughter innocently asked, "Mom, why didn't *you* just give me a tissue?" She was on to me.

This was *not* one of my perfect days. I kissed her minty nose, hugged her goodbye, and whispered in her ear, "Smile today. You got this."

Collapsing into my office chair, ready to reflect on where my morning had gone so wrong, I took a good gulp of my hot caramel latte. It's hot! I choked. Soon I was laughing, sputtering, and snorting whipped cream out of my own left nostril. I reached for a tissue and remembered the words I'd just said to my daughter. "Smile. You got this!" Actually I did. Life was not, is not, and never will be perfect. I'm good enough and I got this.

To this day our not-so-perfect picture-day reminds me to slow down, watch my breathing, rely on help, and keep an eye out for the simple solutions that are often right under my nose. Perfect is an illusion. Bring tissues wherever you go!

Motherhood is the greatest thing, and the hardest thing.

—RICKI LAKE

Yvonne F. Conte

Yvonne Conte is a former award-winning sales executive. She has spent the past twenty-eight years studying the benefits of humor, laughter, and joy. Today she is a nationally recognized corporate culture expert, motivational keynote speaker, and author, helping *Fortune* 500 companies create a positive corporate climate where laughter and humor is encouraged and productivity soars. Connect with her at www.YvonneConte.com, on Facebook at facebook.com/YvonneConteMotivationalSpeaker, on Twitter at twitter.com/YvonneConte, at LinkedIn at linkedin.com/in/yvonneconte/, or call 315.727.8668.

Seven Things My Father Taught Me About Success

Yvonne F. Conte

In 1947 my father became an entrepreneur. Stepping outside the norm, he built a very lucrative business selling stainless steel cookware in Upstate New York. His winning attitude and welcoming smile were some of his greatest assets. People *wanted* to do business with him.

With no formal education or experience, my father built a successful sales organization of over 100 men. He quickly went from barely being able to pay his rent to owning beautiful mansions in New York state and South Florida. That in itself is to be admired, however the most important part of his story is that he did this as a 100-percent disabled World War II veteran fighting the chronic pain of rheumatoid arthritis, an incurable and debilitating disease. He became so successful, in fact, that Utica Mayor John McKennan proclaimed September 8, 1956, to be Frank W. Conte Day, stating that "courage and perseverance under the stress of great hardship are to be admired."

As a little girl I was mesmerized watching my dad work. Sitting quietly next to him on his sales calls, I carefully listened to him connect and communicate with others. On the drive home we would discuss his products, his clients, and his love of people. He was an amazing salesman and a great teacher. Along the way, I learned a great deal about being a successful entrepreneur.

My father credited much of his success to seven basic principles:

1. **Educate Yourself**
   Dad knew how the pots and pans were made. He knew why they were made that way. He knew how cooking in them made for a healthier lifestyle, and he could talk about it with a college professor or engineer with the greatest of confidence. Know your product or service inside and out. Be able to answer

any question that may come up. Continue to read about your industry and your competition and keep current on trends.

2. **Be a Person of Integrity**
   One of the greatest lessons my father taught me is that people with integrity have nothing to hide and nothing to fear. When you do what is right and just, when you tell the truth, when you make right decisions, when you have no ulterior motive, you are a person of integrity. While some unscrupulous people may make a quick buck, their fortune usually doesn't last long after their clients discover their shadiness and stop doing business with them. A person of integrity can be trusted to always look out for your best interest and that is the person who will succeed.

3. **It's Not About You**
   The first thirty minutes of any interaction Daddy had with a customer was full of laughter and chit-chat. Dad wanted to know about his client's family, farm, car, or anything else that was important to him. Everyone seemed to want to be Dad's friend. People loved him. They treated him like a superstar. Dad made others feel important. He talked about them, he asked about them, he wanted to know what they were interested in. He was curious to find out what they needed and what was important to them. Daddy never *sold* anyone on anything. He merely gave them what they needed and wanted.

4. **Help Others Succeed**
   Never be afraid of helping others to succeed. Zig Ziglar said, "You can have everything in life you want, if you will just help other people get what they want." My father lived by that rule. He was interested in teaching other people to sell that cookware the way that he did. He was never afraid to give away his secret to success.

5. **Build Relationships**
   He sold to generations. Customers would call my dad and order sets of cookware for their daughters and sons and, in some cases, grandchildren. A great many of his customers were from referrals. Dad never forgot a name and he never stopped connecting with people. When you have a relationship with someone, you will be the first person they call when they consider buying again.

6. **Love Your Product**
   Dad loved his stainless steel cookware. He believed stainless steel was the only way to go. He was a great cook and could

talk to anyone about cooking, food, and health, all topics he loved and topics that had a lot to do with his bottom line. His was a healthy way to cook. He truly wanted everyone to have these pots because they were the best. Make a note of why you love your product or service. You can't sell anything for long if you don't believe in it and love it.

7. **Be Grateful**
   Finally, I remember that my father was continually grateful for what he had. He was constantly thankful for his children, his family, his ability to work and earn a living. He never dwelled on the negative things in life, instead looking to the positive with a great gratitude.

My father remained 100 percent disabled until his death in 1995, but his positive attitude and love for others never wavered. He was a truly great man whose influence gave me a strong, solid basis on which to live my life, both professionally and personally.

Four Things Real Estate Mogul and Business Expert Barbara Corcoran Taught Me

Yvonne Conte

When we think "shark tank" we think vicious, heartless, ruthless and cold. In truth, my opinion of *Shark Tank* star Barbara Corcoran is just the opposite.

I met her at a WISE (Women Igniting the Spirit of Entrepreneurship) Conference. I was privileged to spend 30 minutes with the woman who turned a $1,000 loan into a multibillion dollar business. Barbara was the keynote speaker and shared her knowledge of business and success on the platform. However, it was at the authors' table I shared with her that really showed me who the woman behind the pink suit and bright lights really was.

When she sat down next to me, she took the time to shake my hand and introduce herself (as if I didn't know who she was). She immediately made me feel I had every right to sit beside her. As the line formed in front of her, she kicked off her high heels and went to work. She signed autographs, took pictures, and accepted gifts from the mile-long line of people waiting for their turn with the Mogul. She was as gracious and kind to the last woman as she was with the first, giving each one her full attention and beautiful smile. When one women proceeded to hold up the line telling Barbara a very long story about her new invention, Barbara sweetly asked her to step to the side and said, "I'm listening and paying full attention, please continue." Then she proceeded to smile and sign a book for the next in line.

In the 30 minutes we shared she was given at least 25 gift bags from her fans. She turned to me and whispered, "They're not really gifts; they're products hoping to be the next big thing," and then she winked at me. She told me she takes them all home with her and has someone look them over. I wondered if the ladies in line knew exactly how lucky they were to have the opportunity to showcase their products to a women who had the power to make them into millionaires.

Barbara Corcoran had every right to act like a diva. She could have demanded in her contract to have special bottled water waiting for her at the table. She could have left the moment her contracted time was met. She had the right to say "No pictures, please," and could have asked for an assistant to help her at the book table to keep the crazies away, but she didn't do any of that. Instead, she made us all fall in love with her by being kind, gracious, interested, and genuine.

The advice she shared in her keynote wasn't much different from the advice I had heard several years ago from CEO Jack Welsh. It didn't surprise me that these two very powerful people had the same ideas about success in business. It was what I learned after her keynote that will stay with me. That is, to always be kind, gracious, interested, and genuine. In my opinion, that's what makes Barbara Corcoran a hero and someone to aspire to.

When I went to leave, I handed her my latest book and said, "Something for you to read on the plane." She not only thanked me, she hugged and kissed me goodbye! She made me feel like we were dear old friends. Barbara Corcoran knows how to make life-long fans. I loved her!

Answered Questions

Yvonne Conte

W hile she slept, I watched her breath. Her small body moving a bit with each intake of air, and I questioned everything. Will I be able to take care of her if she gets sick? Will I make the right choices? Will I be too strict? Not strict enough?

I waited quietly while she danced the ballet and wondered, *Was I patient? Did she eat enough today? Am I a good example?*

With every birthday and Christmas was I honoring her or spoiling her? Would she learn to be gracious and generous or expect to have everything given to her?

What was I teaching her about men, trust, love? Should I let her watch that show, go to that movie, have that experience?

You never really know when you're a mom if you're doing it right. You just do it and hope and pray it will all work out in the end.

With the beauty and elegance of a princess, she picked up her simple bouquet of white daisies and opened the door. A strong, confidant, generous, kind woman walked toward me, reached out, and hugged my neck. "This is the happiest day of my life," she whispered. "Thank you, Momma"

And with those few words the wondering was over.

Lisa A. Joseph

Lisa A. Joseph, MSN, ARNP, FNP-BC, has been a health care professional since 1986, becoming a Nurse Practitioner in 2015, and currently working in hospice care. Lisa is a health care contributor to Lee Health, the largest health-care system in southwest Florida, and *News-Press*, a daily paper in Fort Myers. She has been a featured speaker for the Susan G. Komen Pink Promise Luncheon and is a soon-to-be-certified yoga teacher.

Pause and Situate Yourself

Lisa A. Joseph

Oh my God! Did he just say cancer? He must be in the wrong room. I think he just said my name. Oh, God, he is still talking . . . so it must be me. How do I tell my kids? How will I finish school? How do I pay for all of this? Am I going to die? Biopsy tomorrow. Okay, that will prove him wrong.

I was a forty-seven-year-old single mother of three children, fourteen-year-old twins, and a twenty-seven-year-old son in the military. I was a graduate nursing student, and an as-needed ICU nurse working on my master's degree to become a nurse practitioner. I had always taken care of my health. I had received my routine mammogram five months earlier, funded by Partners for Breast Cancer Care through a Komen grant.

A biopsy was done the day after I received my diagnosis. The pathology report showed infiltrating inflammatory ductal carcinoma. In lay terms this meant I had a very large, aggressive tumor that caused inflammation of the breast and surrounding tissue.

So, now what? Lee Health System's breast health navigator, Tammy Zinn, and the health care team helped me understand what was happening. I was concerned about my health and yet very troubled by the fact that I had no health insurance. I knew the cost of the treatment would be enormous. There were many diagnostic tests that I needed—Mediport placement, breast MRI, PET scan, and echocardiogram. Tammy encouraged me to apply for the Susan G. Komen grant, which provided people in need with the financial support during their breast cancer treatments.

The initial diagnosis was stage-three breast cancer, meaning that the cancer was large and had spread into my lymph nodes. It wasn't until after the PET scan that we found out that it was actually stage-four breast cancer. It had spread past the lymph nodes and was encroaching into my right lung.

I knew that when I was told it was stage three it didn't sound or feel right to me. I could somehow sense it. I cried a lot. Then I made a decision to do whatever it takes to get through this, and I put my full trust and faith into my health care team. I also had the support of my family, friends, co-workers, and classmates. I prayed a lot and used humor as a healing tool whenever I could.

With no health insurance and living on student financial aid, finances were on my mind. Chemo is very expensive and my treatments included three different chemo drugs every twenty-one days for six sessions, with each session costing over $30,000. I was so grateful to Komen for covering my initial treatment costs. Later on I transitioned to Medicaid. There was one drug called Adriamycin. Pretty name for such a potent drug, and it's very thick. The nurse had to hand-push it into the port, taking over ten minutes. I visualized the chemo as a white light going into my blood vessels, dissolving the cancer from my body. There was a second wave of white light that removed it completely, and a third wave that completely healed and cured me. My prayer at night, and while lying on scan and radiation tables, was THANK YOU, THANK YOU, THANK YOU FOR MY HEALING. THANK YOU, THANK YOU, THANK YOU FOR MY CURE.

The day after my first chemo treatment my former hard and firm breast tissue was soft and pliable. It was already working. I felt so hopeful. The thirteenth day after my first chemo, I was in the shower washing my hair and getting ready for my class. Suddenly I had two full handfuls of hair. I stood there for a moment, looked at the hair, and started to cry. Reality was setting in. I prayed that there would be enough hair left on my head so I could get through my class and, with the right amount of hairspray, I managed to pull it off.

My long, beautiful hair was soon completely gone, so I looked for other ways to feel feminine. I went to a makeup class and learned how to make it look like I had eyebrows and eyelashes. I also wore turbans with sequins. I decided I was going to sparkle in spite of the cancer.

My mother was a great help to me emotionally and physically in the weeks that followed. She stayed with me for seven weeks during my chemo, cooking, cleaning, and doing grocery shopping for me. One day while we were watching television together, the *Dr. Phil* show came on. I looked at my mother and said, "Even Dr. Phil has more hair than I do!" We stopped and looked at each other and burst into laughter. Moments like this helped to lift my spirit.

I kept my children informed of my progress. Right at the outset, they wanted to know if they should give up sports and after-school activities. I told them, "Absolutely not! Life goes on, so we'll live our lives as before." I just needed to rest more and balance things out.

At Lee Health System, co-workers took up a collection for me, and because of it, I was able to recover without financial worries. In addition, I was offered a newly created full-time position with benefits. I was able to go to radiation treatments Monday through Thursday and work Fridays, Saturdays, and Sundays.

After my sixth round of chemo it was time for the bilateral mastectomy. My health care team did a lymph node mapping just prior to surgery. Nothing lit up! No lymph nodes were harmed! The pathology report gave me a clean bill of health. Wow! The chemo worked!

After my recovery from surgery I was excited to get back to living my life. I completed my final class, graduated, and passed my nursing boards as a Family Nurse Practitioner. Despite my challenges, I fulfilled my goals only one year later than planned.

Because of generous people and organizations like Susan G. Komen, I am alive today and my life continues. June 20, 2017, was my third-year mark, and I am now considered cured.

Every day is a gift!

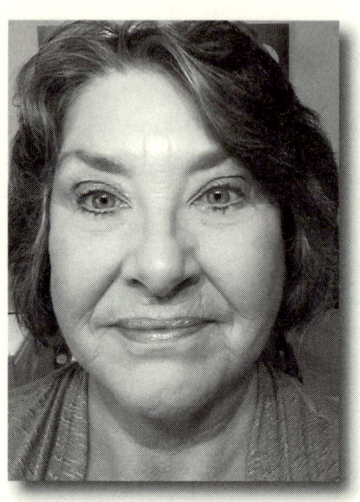

Cindy Ferguson

Cindy Spencer Ferguson is a member of the board of directors of the Day of Joy, Inc. She has a passion to lift up and encourage women of all ages, and has been a volunteer with the organization since its inception in 2010. She serves on the prayer team and intercessory prayer team at the Vineyard Church in Syracuse, NY, where she has been a member for twenty-five years. Her passion for helping people to see their value and heal emotionally has been the encouragement for her to lead small groups using the books *Boundaries*, by Dr. Henry Cloud and Dr. John Townsend, and *The Search for Significance*, by Robert McGee. She has also led Bible studies and, when not leading, enjoys participating. Cindy is a retired medical biller who worked for forty years before disabilities caused her to discontinue working outside the home. She keeps busy with her four grandchildren, a rescue dog named Izzy, lots of word games, aquatic exercise, and creative writing. She is currently working on her first novel.

Hope for the Future

Cindy Ferguson

In the spring of 1968 I was ten years old and had little hope for my future. One would never have guessed this by looking at my home on a beautiful, suburban, tree-lined street. Our property was nicknamed "God's Little Acre" when it went on the market in 1973. Our huge, white, Tudor-style home sat on well kept grounds with tall pines, fragrant magnolias, and giant oaks. My parents and maternal grandparents bought the house in 1962 and, along with my brothers and a sister, lived together as an extended family.

My youngest brother's birth in April, 1967, was a traumatic experience for my mother. He was a breach baby and the obstetrician didn't do a caesarean section. Shortly after his birth she began experiencing weird symptoms she called "spells." My father and I couldn't comprehend what she was experiencing. I thought spells were something witches put on other people. Her illness was later diagnosed as paranoid schizophrenia, something we knew little about. I only remember her being labeled as "crazy." She had delusions of grandeur, others of horror. She was in and out of psychiatric hospitals for years.

During that time my dad was battling alcoholism. I was unaware of this at the time. Later he told me he had hidden his drinking, at least around the house. I could always sense my mother's anxiety when he was out playing golf, because, inevitably, he would come home drunk. This created a sense of instability and fear and I was forever trying to make things better for everyone. I comforted my mom when dad was drunk and helped dad take care of my siblings when mom was in the hospital. I wanted to protect the younger ones. I felt a great sense of responsibility at a very young age, especially after my grandparents moved out.

I experienced the stigma of her mental illness and his alcoholism as if I was stricken with these illnesses myself. I didn't know how to separate my own life from that of my parents. There was shame. I was shy and often withdrawn. Even though my dad brought us to church every Sunday, the love God poured out on me could not penetrate the hard shell I had placed around my heart to keep out all of the bad things that surrounded me.

My teenage years were tumultuous. One day Mom became violent and went after my dad with a butcher knife, putting her hand through the living room window. Dad, who was not injured, was in Alcoholics Anonymous and had been sober for a short time. I watched as my mom was taken by the sheriff to be committed to the mental hospital. I became afraid of her. She was released a few days later because another patient had beaten her up for staring at her. We noted that the medications made her behavior worse. Even though we lived in fear when she came home, she had never become violent like that again.

As I came closer to graduating from high school I wondered how I would ever succeed in life. Would I become like my mother? Like my father? Where could I gain the self-confidence I needed to go to college? Could I leave home when everyone needed me? Where would my hope come from?

Well, my hope came from the Lord. He had been seeking me out all my life. He was with me even during those tumultuous years. I had to finally admit that I could not control anything. I needed the Lord in my life. I could not rescue people because I needed to be rescued. He rescued me when I was thirty-two years old, and I have been a disciple of Jesus ever since. I have learned so much about myself and about maintaining healthy boundaries. I read scriptures, I pray, I listen to His voice, and in this way I learn who Jesus is. I have thrown away the shield that protected my heart, to allow in all that is good and, when necessary, I put the shield back up to keep out all that is bad. I intercede on others' behalfs because He made me with a heart of compassion.

Life is not always easy but if I can do nothing else, I can pray—to the One who bends down and hears my prayers. He can be trusted with my life and with the lives of my family and friends. I no longer question where my hope is. Instead I hold on to the verse in Jeremiah 29:11 which reads:

"For I know the plans I have for you," declares the Lord, "plans to prosper you and not to harm you, plans to give you a hope and a future."

I don't know these plans, but I can hold on to His promise to prosper me and give me hope for the future!

**May He grant
you your heart's
desire and fulfill
all your plans.**

—Psalms 20:4

Tracy DeGraaf

Tracy DeGraaf is a Christian author, speaker, and stand-up comedian entertaining audiences in churches, non-profit organizations, and corporations around the country. She and her husband Ron (aka Muffin) live in the Chicago area with their family. You can visit her website and contact her at www.TracyDeGraaf.com.

Time Waits for No One

Tracy DeGraaf

66 Time waits for no one." That haunting phrase was engraved in my brain while growing up. It was my mother's favorite verbal chant.

It was a Saturday morning in 2005, two weeks prior to my fortieth birthday, officially climbing over that proverbial hill. I went about my cleaning routine, gathering an insane amount of dirty clothes from my hubby, our five sons, and me, and piled it high in the laundry room, wishing I had the courage to launch my own Christian nudist camp. I even had a name for it: Adam and Eve's and No Leaves. But I digress.

On that day I passed by a photo that has been sitting on my dresser for years. It was taken at my wedding in 1989 and shows my husband Ron (I call him Muffin) and me with our parents. I'd walked past that photo countless times, but this time was different. I stopped and looked closely at the picture and focused intensely on my mother. Then I looked at myself in the mirror, then back to my mother. That's when my Aha! moment hit me: "Time waits for no one!"

I got married at 23. My mom was 47 and had just been diagnosed with terminal cancer. Sadly she died at 51 and, in my mind, my mother never aged beyond that point. One of the last things I did with my mom was play cards. It was a few days before she died. She was bedridden but alert, and could still move her hands. She was on regular doses of morphine for pain and we all knew she was in her final days.

When I'd walked in, she smiled and picked up a deck of cards and said, "Let's play rummy, Tray. I want to do therapy with my hands." All she had left was her mind and her hands. I shuffled the cards, tapped the deck, and we played several hands.

I would forever carry that moment with me as inspiration to do the best I can with what I have, because "time waits for no one!" The real kicker was that she was cheating at rummy. She denied it, of course, but the bottom line was that, yep, she was cheating. I called her out on it, but she just chuckled like a little girl caught with her hands in the cookie jar. We both had a much-needed laugh. That was the last time I saw my mother in a conscious state.

Back to 2005. I was a middle-aged woman with a basket of dirty laundry hanging off my hip and I realized: Time really doesn't wait, and if there's something I want to do, I'd better get busy doing it.

That was it. "I'm writing my book!"

Muffin bought me a laptop for my fortieth birthday. At first I thought I'd write a J. K. Rowling–type of novel. But just like in my real life, I couldn't keep track of the characters. A few of my good friends knew I was pursuing my dream of writing a book, and suggested I write about the antics of raising five boys. I had a plethora of material. And that's how my book, *Laugh Anyway Mom*, was born. It's a hilarious collection of stories about Muffin and me surviving our five sons. A publishing coach read my book and advised me to pursue stand-up comedy and I took that advice. Today I travel around the country sharing my one-woman show, "Life Happens; Laugh Anyway", with churches, non-profit organizations, and corporations.

What have you always wanted to do? What's stopping you from doing it? Time waits for no one!! Blessings!!

If you want to do anything, do it now, without compromise or concession, because you have only one life.

—GAO XINGJIAN

Todd Panek

Todd Panek is a husband, father, business professional, and grown-up geek. He is a writer, speaker, and business professional. He writes about a variety of topics on his website TMPinSYR.com, and co-hosts *The SuperPodHeroCast*, available on Podbean, iTunes, or just about anywhere else podcasts are found.

Knowledge Is Power; One to Grow On; The More You Know

Todd Panek

From Francis Bacon to public service announcements, knowing things has always seemed like the secret to success for me. As a student I had wonderful teachers. When I first entered the workforce, I noticed that my bosses who had everything under control also had an easy confidence—they knew everything about their business. During my time in the military, the NCOs and officers whom I admired always had the right answer to whatever it was we were doing. These were the kinds of leaders who left a mark on me.

That must be it. Knowledge is the key. Want to be a great leader in whatever you're doing? It's all about knowing things.

When I was hired into my first leadership role after the military, I was determined to be the kind of leader I admired. I would be that person standing at the front with all of the answers and unwavering confidence. I did everything I could to get the answers, to know things.

After the first survey of my folks, I was disappointed to learn that although I was working hard to know things, it wasn't translating to effective leadership. I was making progress at having the answers but it was clear my people weren't seeing me as the kind of leader I wanted to be. When my boss came to visit the next time, we sat down to talk about the survey results.

Larry was a great boss. He was the perfect person to help me make the transition from military to civilian life. He'd been a naval officer before joining the civilian corporate world. He laid it out plainly. I was not getting it done as a leader. Then he gave me the best advice anyone has ever given me to help me become the most effective leader I can be: "Teach your people to take your job away from you."

Knowledge, I came to understand, is not reduced by being shared. It spreads. It multiplies. And in doing so, it makes for stronger teams.

I approached work as if someone had removed blinders from my eyes. Things clicked. My job became growing as a leader by helping my people grow into their own potential. Whenever I learned something new that helped me, I couldn't wait to share it. "Here! Look at what someone showed me! See how much easier this is? You try it. Great, right?"

I was transformed, invigorated, and I found what would become a passion for me in my career: Helping people develop. This was my new religion and I approached it as fervently as any convert.

Almost magically, my team got stronger. Of course, it wasn't magic. But for me then, it might as well have been. We got better results. My folks were more engaged. I experienced the magic I was aspiring to. I became a leader in deed as well as name.

I'm sure that anyone who has worked in a leadership position has plenty of tough stories: the bureaucratic drag of the administration of human resources, or the unforgettable instances in which a leader had to fire someone. I see these pieces as the other side of the coin, the karmic balance against the very best part of the job of leading people.

When I talk about leadership I go to my happy moments as a leader. I have been privileged to help people get to better places. I'm proud to have helped someone take a step up. Those moments when someone on my team has succeeded and differentiated themselves based on their performance. If I helped someone get there, then I hold onto those moments. Those are my magic experiences as a leader. They make all of the disheartening scenarios nothing more than passing memories. And it all started with giving things away as fast as I could teach them.

Knowledge *is* power, and when you share it, knowledge becomes even more powerful.

So teach your people to take your job away from you.

Waste no more time arguing about what a good man should be. Be one.

—MARCUS AURELIUS

Bruno Schirripa

At age seven, Mother Superior suggested Bruno was much better suited for the public school system, and so his comedy career began. In 1979 he and four partners opened their first comedy night club. Later that same year, the group opened four more comedy rooms. Bruno began his stage career as the emcee for each show, floating club to club. An investment banker offered Bruno an opportunity to open his fourth and fifth comedy clubs in some properties he owned in San Antonio, TX. While there, he acquired top-security clearance at U.S. air force bases so that he could produce shows on base. His sixth and final club and his own TV show, "Wise Guys Tonight," aired for eight seasons, earning five ACE nominations in Syracuse, NY. In 2008 he retired from the comedy clubs and is currently a motivational speaker who focuses on helping teens make better decisions. His greatest joys are being a husband and a father. Contact Bruno at step2bruno@yahoo.com or 315.395.3102.

Precision and Pride in Your Work

Bruno Schirripa

I grew up in Carnegie, PA, near Pittsburgh. My parents migrated to this country from Calabria, Italy. Mom was just a toddler, Dad a teenager. They were raised with old-country values and principals, back when a child couldn't sue his parents for a spanking. It was a time of respect for your elders, respect for authority, and this bred self-respect. Traditional to Italian customs, the first born in our family was named after my father's father. My older sister had that distinction. Her name is Carla as my grandfather was Carlo. I am second in the birth order and named after my mother's father, Bruno. My family calls me "Bruno Duo," meaning Bruno Number Two.

One Saturday morning when I was a teenager, I was asked to help my grandfather dig his garden. My plan was to head down at 9 A.M. as he asked, blow through the digging, and be out in the streets by 11:00. When I arrived, Grandpa informed me that digging the garden meant the entire yard, including terracing the hillside, as he did in Italy. With a pitchfork and brief instruction, I began pounding through at a fever pitch, determined to be done in two hours. After fifteen minutes I developed my first blister. I stopped to catch my breath and looked over at Grandpa who was slowly and steadily working away while giving worldly advice. I noticed he had done quite a bit more than me. I continued to work with vigor. Within five minutes I stopped to catch my breath and get a bandage for my blister. Grandpa, still digging away at the same pace, was making tremendous progress on his half of the yard.

I continued working as hard and as fast as I could, but soon realized it was not the best way to dig. My grandfather masterfully plunged his pitchfork into the ground, turned the earth, and hit the clumps. Finally it sank in. I had to pace myself. I dug in unison with Grandpa. He stopped, looked up at the sun, and said, "Okay, lunch time." We went in the house and washed up. He gave me bread, cheese, pepper, and tomato. We took our lunch out to the back porch to enjoy and survey what we had completed. He said to me, "When you're in a hurry you make mistakes, get tired, and angry. When you work steady, you make efficient movement and finish. You have to do it one time because there are no mistakes." Adapting this philosophy to my everyday life has made me tremendously productive in all that I choose to do.

Be the Best You Can Be

Bruno Schirripa

Dad worked hard. He owned an insurance agency and was on the road most of the week. On weekends he came to my baseball games and encouraged me. He never offered advice unless he was asked. He let us make mistakes, as long as we were not getting hurt or hurting someone. And he was to the point when he spoke.

One of my most memorable talks with dad was while doing yard work. I was in high school with no mention of college or a plan beyond high school. Dad asked me what I was thinking. I said I wanted to continue to work in the grocery store and one day own my own. His advice to me rings in my head every day. "Son, it is not important what you do in your life, just do it the best that you can. If you want to be a garbage man, be the best garbage man anyone has ever seen; if you want to be a policeman, then be the best policeman anyone has ever seen, and no one can ever say anything bad about you. They will say 'Hey, there goes that Bruno Schirripa, I don't like him very much, but he is a good worker.' " He also said, "Make sure you take care of your name; it's the only thing you have to take through this life."

Every day I look in the mirror and remind myself to take care of my name. It's also my father's name, and my sons' name. I walk out my door everyday with my head high and my shoulders back ready to be the best I can be.

Just Do It!

ꞵBruno ꞵSchirripa

My wrestling coach—a great motivator—was a 1969 National Champion. He had a lot of sayings that made it fun to do impressions of him when he was not around. "No guts, no glory" was my personal favorite. Being an overachiever and driven to excel, my work ethic was extreme. If you've ever watched Greco-Roman wrestling, you know it's just you and your opponent for six full minutes. Every ounce of energy you have is on the mat in front of a crowd screaming for you.

I felt I was not giving all that I had. I loved the feeling of being on the mat, exerting myself, and really working hard to make each movement work. I grimaced and strained, but often, some of the things I did were not effective.

In talking with Coach Guidi in practice, he said a few words to me that have stuck in my head and I employ to this day: "Bruno, trying to do a move and doing the move are very different. While going through motions and straining you're doing nothing more than spending time and energy making it look like you're doing something. If you truly want it, then just do it." That is so true about most of us. We go through a lot of motion trying and that is all we are doing . . . trying. When you're only trying, you haven't truly committed to success; you have committed only to *try* to succeed. In a way, you're making it okay to fail. His words became part of me and in my life I applied his advice, and it works!

Belief Is the Spirit Within You

Bruno Schirripa

On my thirty-second birthday I was in a store buying clothes. I happened to walk by a mirrored pillar and noticed a horrifying image. I stopped and backed up to take another look. Back in my wrestling days, my weight was 105; my weight that day was 201! I ran from the store, sat in my car, and cried. Having suffered limited mobility from a neck injury ten years before had taken its toll on my mind, body, and spirit. I dried my eyes and opened a conversation with God. I was committed to make a change that day. I never lit another cigarette and my drug habit ended at that moment. I began to eat the way I did when I was at my peak physical condition. I needed to work on healing my physical injuries.

I'd read that through the practice of martial arts I might lessen the excessive strain that my previous injuries had caused to my body. I walked into a Tae Kwon Do school and met Grand Master Sun Ki Chong, three-time Korean national champion. I explained my situation and physical difficulties. He said he could help. I began training in Tae Kwon Do and also sought the care of a chiropractor who specialized in athletic injuries. After two visits I went two full days free of pain for the first time in ten years. Over the next six months I strengthened my neck muscles to alleviate the pain of the injury and became more proficient at Tae Kwon Do. My mind and body where rebuilding and my spirit was regaining strength.

I felt so good and strong that I wanted to try sparring. My doctors had told me that I could never compete again due to the severity of my neck injury, and even though I'd been training in Tae Kwon Do for only six months, I seriously wanted to enter a full-contact competition. At the weigh-in, I tipped the scale at 178 pounds. This qualified me as a welterweight, tall and thin and a bit more mobile than heavyweight fighters. I faced my opponent and felt really good about my movement and ability to get in and score, even though he was at least a foot taller. However, at the end of the bout the referee raised the hand of my opponent. I was beaten by one point. But I was happy and grateful that I was pain-free and had mobility and desire to compete. I didn't like that I'd lost, though, so I trained harder and grew faster and stronger. Over the next three years I competed several times, each time winning by a larger margin. As I grew stronger physically I grew stronger mentally and spiritually.

The invitation to the U.S. National Championships was posted on the wall of my Tae Kwon Do school—Black Belt division only. I wore a red belt, which is just before the black belt. I asked Grand Master Chong to make an exception for me and qualify me as a Black Belt so I could compete. He tried to reason with me, saying that sparring with younger fighters was not a good idea. I was thirty-five at the time. My injury had healed, my mind was strong, and my spirit stronger. After some discussion I received my promotion to Black Belt.

Grand Master Chong asked me, "Are you sure you are ready to be doing this?"

"Sir," I answered, "God has given me another chance—an opportunity to finish something I started. I'm ready to claim my prize."

Training for this event was very much like what I used to do when I wrestled. I've always "emptied the tank" in training so I'd know how much is left when I'm in competition. I also trained with fighters much bigger than I. My thought was that no one in my division could hit me as hard as they did, and it made me faster so I could avoid being hit. My focus and drive were clear. My last training session before leaving for competition was full-gear sparring. My training partner and I bowed and readied. He bowed again and stepped back exclaiming, "I looked into your eyes and saw a very scary animal glaring back at me." Indeed I was a scared animal. Martial arts movements are designed and performed to resemble elements and animals. Wind, fire, water, earth. I would be a panther and show him! I once had a T-shirt with the slogan "LEAVE NO DOUBT." My goal was to be so decisively the victor that there would be no way the wrong hand would be raised in victory.

The flight arrived in Madison at 6 P.M. and I went straight to the weigh-in at 7. Many fighters had to lose weight to make their qualifying division. It was common to weigh-in wearing very light weight compression shorts or undergarment. My division was called and the fighters began to strip down. I walked forward to the scale set at the highest qualifying weight for my division—135, flyweight. I stated my name and stepped on the scale, fully clothed, sweatshirt and T-shirt under it, ball cap, workout pants, shoes, socks, and my

Walkman. I had lost 66 pounds on my way to regain the opportunity I had missed years before. I was confident that I would leave Wisconsin with my prize. I believed that with every fiber of my existence. Every day at the end of my training session I employed a system of focus called guided imagery. I would stand with my eyes closed and raise my arms in victory, imagining I was on the top of the podium with a gold medal around my neck, the crowded arena cheering and applauding. It was going to happen just that way.

The next morning I woke early, had a little breakfast, and a good warm-up session before heading to the arena. My division was up first. When I walked into the arena an amazing energy came over me. I had never felt so empowered in my competitive career as I did at that moment.

I changed, got ready to fight, and headed to the ready room, where everyone in your division is held until they're paraded out to the competition area like gladiators into the coliseum. While most others hit targets with punches and kicks, working off nervous energy, I sat in a corner of the room with my eyes closed, visualizing myself moving with freedom and grace, power and efficiency. I was becoming the panther. I was ready.

I stood on the ring apron with my coach. Grand Master Chong approached me and, as my wrestling coach had done, gave me words of encouragement. In his gentle, yet commanding voice he said, "Go show them who's your daddy!" A black belt for only five days, I entered the ring and noticed the grayed belt of my opponent and three stripes indicating that he is a third-degree black belt.

The bout began, and he attacked quickly with a punch that caught me on the left side of my chest. I immediately responded with a strong kick, finding its mark on his midsection, causing him to back off a little. This gave me a chance to get far enough away from him so that he couldn't hear me gasping for air. His punch had cracked a rib and taken my breath away. I felt my spirit start to float away as the pain from the injury set in. Seconds felt like hours, but if I stopped to catch my breath, the pain might show on my face and the bout would stop. I would be assessed by the ring doctor, receive an automatic eight-count for stopping, the match would end, and the gold medal would go to my opponent. I refused to let my spirit leave. I proceeded to pound on my opponent for the remainder of the round. The first time I went to my corner between rounds, my coach knew something was wrong, so I told him. He wanted to stop the bout, but I stood up, bowed to him, and walked to the center of the ring to start the next round.

Through the second round I countered my opponent's punching ability with swift movements off his line of attack and kicks to his side. I was able to score heavily. He made some adjustments. After throwing a punch he would retract quickly to protect his side from my kick. I would continue to kick but was now hitting his elbow. After a few great shots I had no feeling in my foot as I had crushed the nerve sheathing. My energy level started to dip, but I continued to pursue my opponent. I wasn't going to leave any doubt in anyone's mind who was the champion. The referee stepped in as the round and the bout ended. My opponent and I hugged in the middle of the ring, congratulating each other on a hard-fought battle.

The referee returned with the decision. When my hand was raised and the crowd erupted, I was filled with gratitude and emotion, and I took my place on the top of the podium. As the gold medal was placed around my neck, I raised my arms to cheers and applause from the standing crowd. What was most amazing to me at that moment was the thought that I'd imagined this moment so many times over the past few months of training. It happened exactly the way I saw it in my mind's eye. The big difference was the emotion I felt in the moment. I left the podium and bowed to Grand Master Chong. He returned the bow. I removed the medal from my neck and, with a grand bow, handed it to him. It rightfully belonged to him; I was merely the vessel for his victory. I was humbled by the congratulations I received from the fourteen Grand Masters in his entourage. He then approached me, handing the medal back, and said, "You hold this for us. I know that you will care for it as I would."

I wake up every morning remembering that feeling and take the mind, body, and spirit I created through each day. Every day I strive to move with the precision of a U.S. national champion, with the desire to excel, the drive to produce energy and the heightened spirit necessary to be that champion.

I teach Tae Kwon Do at LeMoyne College in Syracuse, NY. I am a 5th Degree Black Belt Master Instructor and am the head coach for the intercollegiate fighting team. I hold two New York State Governor's Cup Gold Medals, three NYS Championship Gold Medals, and am a U.S. National Tae Kwon Do Champion. Since 1990 I have trained four U.S. national champions and the gratification I felt with each one was just as emotional as if I had stood in the ring myself.

Denise Sherriff

Denise and her son Anthony live in Ooltewah, TN. She was married to Richard Sherriff until his death in 2017. She has a shepherd's heart and perseveres in finding and serving those who need her. Denise says, "Life's experiences have given her the faith of David to slay giants, the strength of Samson to move virtual mountains, and the wisdom like Solomon to make wise choices." Learn about her latest book, *Kairos Moments*, at kairosmoments2017.com. She can be contacted at denisesherriff.com, kairosmoments2017@yahoo.com, facebook.com/kairosmomentsbook, or 423.240.9389.

Be a Champion in Your Life!
It Can't Be Everyone Else

Denise Sherriff

It can't be everyone else. This was the beginning of restoration for me. I hope that, by exposing the ugliness I've been through, I can point someone else in the right direction.

I began attending Restoration Ministries, classes that would take all of me if I were to be changed. I considered myself above and better than those who would need such classes. Yet somehow I knew I needed to stay and fight for my spiritual freedom. I had been rescued from sleeping in the storage room of a home that was being established to help others that were broken. A grandmother, Pearl, took me in. She sat in her rocker every night with me at her feet. I placed my head in her lap. She laid her hand on my head, wiped my tears, and prayed over me. She lovingly prepared meals for me, like I was family. During the day we all had jobs. Some were groundskeepers, others cleaning people, like me. I cleaned the restrooms. I went kicking and screaming into the pastor's office almost daily, but I fulfilled my duties anyway. I learned humility. To this day I'm willing to clean a toilet for anyone, anywhere.

Restoration Ministries was so new, they didn't even have pre-printed material to study. Like a high-spirited horse, I was only partially broken. As long as I wanted to blame others for my indiscretions, getting to the core of my problems would be difficult. I learned a lot in that first year. A major turning point was a teaching on unforgiveness and forgiveness. Unforgiveness was taught first and I opposed this criteria. My hand would go up and the pastor would say, "Denise, put your hand down and listen first." I didn't realize it, but I was holding unforgiveness closer to my heart and mind, as most of us do. I mislabeled it as protection. I learned what happens when we prefer not to forgive. That's why it's taught first. It's the catalyst that shoots us forward in the desire of wanting to forgive.

God began doing a new thing in me. I was being peeled like an onion, layer by layer. I was so full of junk, it's a miracle I didn't explode from all the poison I ingested spiritually. Attending these classes was the most difficult and painful chapter in my life. But it was also the best part of my life and I was changed forever. Those classes helped me see what was going on inside of me. I began hearing without distortion and learned how to operate with more clarity of mind. Simply put, people who hurt hurt others. We can't change anyone else, but we can change ourselves if we want to. After all these years, I often refer to my old notes when I start thinking I have it all together. I definitely have not arrived.

We destroy every proud obstacle that keeps people from knowing God. We capture their rebellious thoughts and teach them to obey Christ.

—2 Corinthians 10:5

Laura Hand

Laura Hand is best known as the news anchor on *Weekend Today in Central New York*, Saturday and Sunday mornings on WSTM, Channel 3, Syracuse. She also anchors and produces WSTM's "Monday Night Answer Desk" segments on the local news. She is a long-time member of The Salvation Army/Syracuse board. She also is passionate about encouraging children to love reading, and for 30-plus years has organized the station's "Book Breaks" summer reading campaign. She is in the process of having her dog certified as a therapy dog, to have children read to her. For the past several years, Laura has emceed the Italian flag raising at Syracuse City Hall, which opens La Festa Italiana. Many people don't realize she spoke Italian before she learned English, and remains fluent in that language. At this past year's Festa she also gave a presentation on Trieste, where she spent her childhood summers, and where she still visits relatives regularly.

The Slap

Laura Hand

It often takes years—sometimes decades—to realize that a seem-ingly insignificant occurrence is a life changer. In this case, it also took a chance occurrence all these years later that made for the realization.

In the late 1950s, my family was living in Hampton, VA. My father, a career Army officer, was being sent on temporary duty for several months, and we could not accompany him. My mother decided to take my baby brother and me to her home in Trieste, Italy. We had spent summers there, but this time it was for part of the school year and she was going to home-school me. Part of the trip preparation was a visit to the Hampton Schools offices, to pick up text books.

After the business visit, we stopped at a downtown department store. It was hot, and I went to get some water at a drinking foun-tain. One of the sales clerks slapped me away. She then explained to my mother that this fountain was for "colored only." We may have been living in the South, but as an Army family we were living in a different and much more integrated society. My mother, Italian, undoubtedly knew little of the "rules" of the time, and did nothing but move me away. I remember thinking it was a lot of fuss over nothing. Water is water.

Fast forward to this past summer, and the movie Hidden Figures, about African American women who were mathematicians, and who had to overcome outright discrimination, but persevered and greatly contributed to our Space Program. The same story—from the other side. In watching, I realized that one long-ago incident made me un-derstand that we all have the same wants and needs, and that some of our neighbors, well intentioned, try to set and enforce rules that are unrealistic and hurtful.

On reflection, I cannot help wondering how many other young people had similar encounters with "well meaning" adults, and came away with the same conclusion, that became ingrained in the way we approach other human beings. In other words, that effort at "protecting" actually made us question, and discard the old beliefs of inequality.

Maybe this is the life lesson: taking a rigid stand is no guarantee of an expected outcome. As people, we are all endowed with intelligence, and if brought up in an environment of caring and compassion, will look past "the rules."

Racism is still with us. But it is up to us to prepare our children for what they have to meet, and, hopefully, we shall overcome.

—ROSA PARKS

Nick Marra

Nick is a stand-up comic, husband, and father. He is a lover of life and laughter. Learn more about him and connect with him at www.funnymannick.com, on Twitter, @my funnymannick, or by email at Nick@funnymannick.com.

The Inspiration of Rick Palermo

Nick Marra

My first real job was at Bob's Big Boy as a manager trainee. I was nineteen and moved two hours from home to take the job in Batavia, NY, where some distant relatives of my father lived. One day my aunt came in to the restaurant to see me and invited me to her home for homemade pasta and meatballs. She told me about her son, Rick, who was paralyzed from the neck down in a horrible accident.

When I met Rick I was a bit nervous. I never met anyone who was paralyzed. Do I shake his hand? Can he shake mine? What do I talk to him about? I walked in, met the entire family, and they were wonderful. In a back room Rick was sitting up in a hospital bed. His mom took me over to meet him. I put out my hand to shake his, but he could only swing his arm and couldn't grip my hand. He immediately said "Relax, Nick, everyone does that. It's no big deal." He made me feel so at ease. After spending three hours with him and his family, I was so comfortable. He wasn't paralyzed. He was just a guy, sitting in a bed.

Over the next several months, Rick and I became close friends. I never heard him complain once. I visited Rick several times a week, going out to lunch and enjoying time with him. He told me I was working too hard and needed to slow down. He has a way of making you feel comfortable and has an incredible attitude. I'm sure he has moments when he's depressed but he's never shown it.

Rick knows I'm a comedian. I love him because he can say anything to me and I can do the same with him. The first time I took him out in his van, I secured his wheelchair with the brake and then wrapped a strap around his chest. "Don't be afraid to pull it tight," he said the first time, so I wrapped it as tight as I could. Only one problem: I didn't wrap it around the back of the chair! When I walked away, he fell forward. I was so embarrassed and felt so bad.

He looked at me and said "You really are an idiot, aren't you?" We both laughed.

"The Miami Project" is his annual golf tournament that raises money to find a cure for paralysis. In twenty years he's raised over one million dollars in a town of about 25,000 people. Every person who attends the tournament makes a connection with Rick. There are no corporate sponsors, just the local community pulling together for him. They raised enough money to buy a special bike that can be operated by brain stimulation. It's at the local YMCA and Rick rides it for 45 minutes, three days a week.

I urge anyone to spend ten minutes with Rick. It will give you a different outlook on life. It has for me. He has inspired me for more than twenty-five years. I pray every day that a cure will be found for his paralysis. His attitude motivates me to never give up, never complain, and to be grateful in all situations

Our chief want is someone who will inspire us to be what we know we could be.

—RALPH WALDO EMERSON

Lisa Cavallaro

Lisa Cavallaro is a master certified coach, certified weight loss coach, and Reiki master. Coaching and supporting parents and kids toward happier, healthier, and more fulfilled lives is her idea of a good time. Lisa is a wife, mother, and grandmother living in Syracuse, NY, and Jupiter, FL. Learn more at www.lisacavallaro.com.

Happiness Is an Inside Job

Lisa Cavallaro

I'm sure your daughter's lovely, but I prefer to work with you.
These were not the words I was looking for. After telling my
new therapist about the difficulties I was having with then eleven-
year-old Marisa, the response I heard from her took me by surprise.
This lady was the second professional I'd been to and came highly
recommended by a professor at Syracuse University, where I was a
graduate student in the Marriage and Family Therapy Department.
My daughter was the main reason I went back to school. I was looking for strategies to help me change her behavior. I wanted to know
why she acted the way she did. More than that, I wanted to put an
end to it.

Marisa and I clashed big time and it was no secret to my husband,
our other two kids, or anyone in our extended family. Typically, our
mother-daughter interactions would go something like this: I'd ask
Marisa to do something. She either wouldn't do it or she'd exclaim a
defiant "No!" I'd repeat myself louder. She'd repeat *herself* louder—
with a foot stomp for added effect. I'd issue some type of punishment. She'd roll her eyes and tell me what a bad mother I was. I'd
threaten with another punishment. Like a merry-go-round—around
and around we'd go.

This frustrating, unproductive pattern would usually continue
until Marisa stomped her feet on her way out of the room and then
slammed her bedroom door. Sometimes Marisa would call my sister
Roseanne to ask if she could go live with her because I was such
an awful mother. (The little smarty-pants would always make sure
I could hear every last word she was saying.) My typical "mature"
response was along the lines of: "Go ahead. There are lots of little
girls who would love to have your bedroom when you leave."

In my mind, Marisa had an attitude problem and although
it started when she was just a toddler, I desperately needed it to
change before she hit those dreaded teenage years. As you might

guess, the therapist really caught me off guard when she said she wanted me to be her client—and not my daughter. I wasn't going down without a fight so I gave this woman even more reasons why Marisa needed her help and I didn't. But she wasn't having it. Either I became the client or I would have to look for a third therapist. The lady won. She backed me into a corner. And honestly, it was the best fight I ever lost.

It's been more than fifteen years since the day my original plan backfired in my face. For a couple of those years, I met with the therapist each month. During the first few sessions I'd still try to sell her on the idea of working with my daughter. Still, she wasn't buying. After a little while, other topics came up. I'd bring my opinions on school, family, career, and life in general. She listened with compassion but she never let me whine. She refused to let me play the victim. Eventually, I came to realize there was nothing wrong with Marisa and she was not pulling defiant behavior out of her hat. My beautiful brilliant daughter was simply responding to me.

That day in the therapist's office was a turning point for me. It was the beginning of my learning to take the finger I was pointing at other people and point that thing at myself. The therapy I reluctantly began taught me a huge lesson: It wasn't Marisa's job to make my life easier or happier and it wasn't the job of any of those other people I may have complained about to that brilliant therapist.

Happiness is an inside job. As one who took years to fully understand this, I know what it's like to drive yourself bonkers waiting for someone else to do your work. My mission to change Marisa's behavior is what turned out to be the catalyst to my own journey of self-discovery, a journey that continues to teach me that I have all that I need and that discovering more ways to use it is where the fun is.

When you're constantly looking for things from other people, you're not looking within yourself.

—SANDRA BERNHARD

Reinhardt Brucker

Reinhardt Brucker was born to Yugoslavian parents in Germany. His family moved to the United States when he was three. His love of music and performing began with violin lessons from his musician father. He plays many instruments, sings, acts, and is a public speaker. His message has always been "How can I make things better for you?" Rein is a professional real estate broker who has helped people find their dream homes since 1977. He is a father of five with two grandchildren and enjoys spoiling his wife. One of his favorite humanitarians, Albert Einstein, once said, "Strive not to be a success, but rather to be of value." His book, *Humblings of an Everyday Man*, can be purchased on Amazon. He can be reached by voice or text at 585.317.4444 or online at www.ReinBrucker.com.

P.S. I'm always honored to receive your referrals!

Mother's Love

Reinhardt Brucker

It was just another Pennsylvania Dutch–type craft show, with hut after hut of fine handiworks. They were like little houses, end to end, in long, neat rows along the street, and each end had a screen door that led to the screen door of the next one. This was apparently done to separate the vendors' individual personalities.

I was carrying one of my clothing purchases on a hanger from one hut to another, browsing. As I exited one shop's screen door to open the next, I looked in to see the back of the saleslady I was about to meet. I froze, stunned in place as I looked at her. It couldn't be! Her back was to me but there she was! She was about 4-10 with a plain farmer's wife–type blouse, skirt, apron, and the perpetual kerchief. She always mispronounced "kerchief" because when we came to America from Germany, Krushchev was in power in Russia. She heard his name, and thinking her headwear was named after him, the term stuck. She always called it her "krushchev." My heart fluttered, a lump formed in my throat, and I began to perspire. I had missed her so much since she died seven years ago. There was so much I wanted to say to her before her debilitating Alzheimer's disease overtook her mind. There were so many regrets of not having called her more frequently, not spending more time with her after Dad died. I got involved with my own life and affairs and lost touch with the fact that she gave me life.

Confusion ricocheted through my brain. Why here? Why now? I couldn't help the urge of wanting to burst through the door and consume her tiny frame with bear hugs. She turned slowly. It wasn't her. She was very close in looks, but it wasn't my Mamma. Not a word was spoken; we just exchanged looks. My face initially showed gleeful anticipation, then regret, then disappointment, all of which were sensed by her immediately. Her life's experiences recognized my emotions instantly, and she wanted to comfort me with her eyes. My eyes saddened. I lowered my head and walked away. I missed my Mamma.

I headed for the nearest tree to sit under and cry. At this moment I missed her so. As I turned to sit, there she was again. She had followed me from her store. As our eyes met she said, "It's really *me*!"

"What?" I said.

"It's really *me*!" she repeated.

"Who?" I asked softly

"Whoever it is you're missing right now," she answered.

"My Mamma," I answered back.

"That's me," she said.

"But you're not her," I softly protested.

"I am for now, God sent me here for you, just for the moment, to comfort you."

I can't explain why I collapsed and dissolved into her arms, sobbing, but she held me as I cried. All my sorrow and regrets spewed out to her in a torrent of emotion . . . to my Mamma.

She listened and comforted me for over an hour, never once thinking about her store. I was, for that hour, once again in my mother's presence, and more important, in my mother's arms.

She gently wiped my tears with the ever-present tissue she carried in every pocket and sleeve, kissed me on the forehead, and said, "I love you and I'm very proud of you. I'm fine. Now go back and continue your wonderful life." With one last motherly hug and kiss, she turned and walked back to her store. That tiny frame with the "krushchev" was once again anchored in my heart. That's when I awoke . . . sobbing. We just never know, do we?

Go Ahead . . . JUMP!

Reinhardt Brucker

It was 1990, the first day of my forced acceptance of the fact that my life as a husband would end. Three days later I was poised to jump. *Go ahead and . . . JUMP! After all, that's what I came up here for, wasn't it?* I was numbed by emotional pain. Was I making a rational decision by jumping? Who knows? Yet, having planned it, I knew I had to go through with it.

Bill was a veteran skydiver and instructor. He talked me into it I told him I wanted to do it. He said, "Sure, that's what they all say." But when I said I would do something, I followed through.

I showed up at the small airport in Batavia, NY, on that bright sunny day to partake of the mega-adrenaline rush that area enthusiasts called skydiving. Not parachuting, mind you, but skydiving. Parachuting was for wimps, I came to learn, but I was to learn so many more things that day.

I had done parachuting years earlier and it was done from 2,800 feet. The little plane I'd gone up in looked more like a reject from an MGM backlot disaster film. It seemed to be held together with spit and chewing gum. After we'd all climbed in, it rattled its way down the dirt runway, parallel to the cow pasture. I felt sorry for the pilot and was elated that I, at that point, was the one with the chute on. When we got up to 2,800 feet our instructor popped open the gullwing door as the pilot slowed the plane to 70 MPH. Hearing the rush of the wind explode in the cabin had me check the dryness of my trousers. My chute had a little strip of Velcro protruding from the top, called a static line. This was attached to another piece of Velcro that was bolted to the floor of the plane. I waited for the jumpmaster to scream "JUMP!" My heart pounded as one foot was on the plane and the other dangled almost 3,000 feet above the earth. I let go of that little rattletrap and my chute was automatically pulled out for me as I fell. It was a tremendous rush.

Today I would be moving from 2,800 feet to 15,000. That's about three miles. Couple that with the fact that my chute would not be opening for almost a full minute. Sounds short, huh? I thought so, too. Stop and count to yourself, "one-one thousand, two-one thousand, three-one thousand," and so on, all the way up to sixty-one thousand. Then further realize that during all that time, you'd be falling toward the earth at 120 MPH. That's like sitting on the hood of a car while going over a cliff and into a canyon three miles deep for (count 'em) 60 seconds.

The reason for today's jump at this location was due to a larger than usual cargo plane being on site, which is a rarity and luxury at the same time. Twenty skydiving enthusiasts were here together, and these crazies jumped out at the same time. With twenty people at a time they could do all those star-like hand-holding formations you see on TV. They even had three or four jumpers with video cameras built into their helmets to film the formations. For an extra thirty bucks I hired one of them to film me. I wanted to make sure my friends believed me when I told them about it.

The instructor told me we'd be doing a tandem jump. That means that the instructor is buckled to my back. I found that New York State laws required me to make about 40 or 50 static-line jumps before they'd allow me to freefall on my own. At about 60–70 bucks a jump, I decided on this shortcut to one of life's ultimate rushes.

You see, the theory is that even if I passed out and didn't pull the ripcord of our two-man, extra-large chute, the instructor, having a personal interest in his own survival, would be my guardian angel. We suited up, harnessed ourselves together, and were shoe-horned into this ultra-light tuna-fish-can-of-a-plane. I was told the skydiver's unspoken rule. Once you have all your equipment strapped on and you're ready, you never land with the plane. "Oh, my God!" I thought. "That means everybody jumps once they're in the air!" I asked how that could be. There had to be some other first-time jumper like me who, at one time or another got to the door of the plane at 15,000 feet, looked down, and freaked out, right? They said that some people do but that they just gently pry their fingers from the fuselage and calm them down, tell them to slowly waddle back into the plane and sit down, then as soon as they turn to walk forward back into the plane, the instructor who's still strapped to their back pulls them backward, falling out the door and into the atmosphere.

"Don't people get a little bit ticked off?" I asked.

"Not really," was the answer. "Once they're all suited up and standing at the door we already know that since they've come this far, they'd be more angry that they *didn't* jump."

I knew right away that these people were a different breed. One woman jumper was even three months pregnant and bragged to me that her baby already had three jumps since inception.

Standing in the plane's arched doorway, looking down at the farm field–quilted earth, I'm sure I was terrified. I thought more than twice about turning around, but remembered that I'd get yanked out the door anyway. Then it hit me: This was the physical mani-festation of a metaphor for what was happening in my life. I was at the edge of a mammoth void. I could turn around and stay in the mundane safeness of the plane and go back to the way things were, but nothing would change. Even worse, nothing would be learned. Or I could trust that by stepping into the void I'd learn things about myself, my life, and the universe.

Today I thirsted for more. All my past learned experiences came together and made me realize that nothing is forever, that the only thing constant in life is change.

"Jump!" said the voice of God inside my head. So I trusted, let go, and stepped into the void. The instructor on my back became my higher self or my God spirit who was watching over me.

This seemingly little step into nothingness was a gargantuan step of learning to trust further than I'd ever trusted before. For the next five seconds my entire being went into sensory overload. I couldn't tell if I was falling, walking, flailing, or flying. Time stood still. The torrent of rushing wind blew into my face, up my nostrils, and into the back of my throat with such force that I thought I'd asphyxiate, but my body adjusted its breathing. By the time I came back to sensing what was happening I was fearfully ecstatic. I looked at the cameraman falling face-to-face across from me. I cheered and whooped but was barely heard. I looked below and saw the tapestry of farm fields growing larger and more colorful. My higher power gently tapped my side three times, the signal to pull the ripcord to open the chute. I clumsily yanked it out of its holder. A magnificent canvas of life-saving color inflated with air above our heads. It slowed our journey between here and earth as the second phase of my jump turned into an amazing and awesome wonderment of awareness. Looking down, my problems seemed so minuscule.

I was elated that I was able to trust something again and everything turned out so right. As we gingerly touched down, I was a different, more peaceful soul, with a knowingness that change, especially rapid and immense change, was God's way of saying, "I believe you're ready to grow to the next level of life. You have learned all the lessons of this period and it is now time for you to change into betterment. You are now ready to learn the next lesson.

Tommy Moore

Tommy Moore is an American comedian, clown, and motivational speaker, versed in the styles of vaudeville and Catskill comedy. Billed as "The Professor of Fun," he has been called the "man who put the FUN back in funny." His latest book, *A Ph.D. in Happiness*, is filled with stories about his experience with famous comedians, including George Burns, Jackie Mason, Jay Leno, Harry Anderson, and Rosie O'Donnell. He can be reached at www.profcomedy.com.

Don't Try Anything Funny!

Tommy Moore

I was in the middle of a robbery. I'd been hit on the head nine times with a pipe and tied up with rope. The robber looked down at me and said, "Don't try anything funny!" I had been a professional comedian for nine years. Never tell a comedian not to be funny! It may have started with the first pie in the face. Tell us we cannot be funny, and that's exactly what we must do. In a pool of blood, and with a gag in my mouth (not the joke kind), I worked my way out of the ropes (I had been a magician as well. Thanks, Harry Houdini!), and was soon in the hospital. They worked diligently, putting 186 stitches in my head (I asked them to sew in some hair plugs, but they declined), and applying casts to my arms and leg. A comedy club owner said that I might never stand on a stage again. I had a show three nights later and I'd never missed a show in my life. I wasn't about to now. In head-to-toe casts and bandages, I did that show! I told lots of doctor jokes that night. I've done over 4,000 shows since, plus speeches, seminars, TV and radio appearances, taught stand-up comedy for five years at Philadelphia's Temple University, and done over 2,500 mini-shows in patient rooms since co-founding The Moore Regional Hospital Clowns. I've traveled to England, Iceland, Germany, Wales, and the Netherlands for the USO, and written two books on comedy (all of them funny!). It's been forty-plus years of making people laugh. "Don't try anything funny?" Ha! I don't think so!

Terri Zbick

Terri Zbick is a retired career counselor/coach who now writes résumés for people in career transition, either by choice or circumstances. She and her husband Joe live in Phoenix, AZ, and Rochester, NY.

Life After Corporate America

Terri Zbick

YOU'RE FIRED! Leaving a job, either through loss of the position or transitioning to retirement can be emotionally challenging as so many of us hang our value on what we do at work.

As a career counselor, I see people in crisis—because they are no longer working. However, I know that finding a meaningful, more fulfilling life—post–job loss—is possible. Many individuals admit to wanting a change prior to their job loss, but needed the jolt of a layoff to pursue a livelihood more compatible with their values.

Some discover life after corporate America by evolving to a different existence, discovering additional skills, and recapturing a zest for living.

A client I will call Alice was in her seventies and had been forced to leave her position. She considered herself too young to be out of the workforce. She had never used a computer, but she'd taken a typing class and had applied to work part-time in her doctor's office.

Another client lost a high-paying corporate position. I met her the day she lost her job and, with it, her self-worth. Later she revealed that her biggest challenge was reconciling the fact that she was happier and more content since losing her job. All of her social input to this point was telling her she should have a job and be accumulating wealth, but her heart was in the economics of helping others and volunteering more, and that is what she transitioned to. The pay was not great, but the peace and contentment was priceless.

Laura was fired from her job. In addition to the emotional trauma of unfairly losing her job, she was struggling with some family issues. Within a very short time, she reported a miraculous turnaround in her family that could only be attributed to reinvesting her 80-hour workweek to time on the home front.

Dave had a passion for ministry, counseling, and helping people. He admitted that he no longer enjoyed his technical position, but the pay was keeping him stuck. He had already transitioned emotionally in that all his free time was spent in religious study, mission trips, or church work. The loss of his job enabled him to assess his situation and realize that it was time for him to put corporate life behind him, use a different set of skills, and focus on new goals. For him this meant finding a ministry and accepting a new lifestyle.

My personal story is that I was not ready to leave my position, but an aging father became more important than holding out for a retirement package. It turned out to be the best decision of my career. I would never have another opportunity to bless him with new experiences and hear his stories and get to really know and love him. After he passed, I realized I was no longer a fit for corporate America and they were no longer a fit for me. In my new lifestyle, I enjoy time with my family and volunteering with my husband.

When you talk to someone who has left a traditional corporate role, rather than ask, "Are you working?" ask, "What are you doing now?" You may be surprised at the answers, and even more surprised at the increased level of happiness and contentment. Look at your own work/life balance and ask if you should make a change that is more conducive with your purpose, ambition, and goals.

The Holy Spirit
produces this kind
of fruit in our
lives; love, joy,
peace, patience,
kindness, goodness
and faithfulness.

—*GALATIANS* 5:22

Thom Rutledge

Thom Rutledge is the author of several books, including *The Greater Possibilities, What Love Is, Embracing Fear,* and *The Self-Forgiveness Handbook.* He is a syndicated columnist, talk-show guest, psychotherapist, and author. Thom lives in Nashville, TN. He can be reached at www.thomrutledge.com.

One Life

Thom Rutledge

My father hated himself. Of course, I had no idea about that when I was a kid. I'm pretty sure I didn't even know that some people hated themselves. I sure didn't know I was moving down that very same road—the road of "No matter what, never good enough."

I loved my father, and still do. People die, but relationships don't, right? From the time I began therapy in my early thirties, it became increasingly clear that one powerful source for the shame and self-condemnation I was beginning to face was the fact that my most important male role model hated himself. It was confusing for me when I began to sort through all of this. My father had always gone out of his way to tell me to be proud of myself. "Do what you love to do," was his career advice. My original career goal was becoming a professional magician and when I let that one go, I was certain that I was going to be a rich, famous, and much celebrated poet. My father supported me in both of those dreams. I don't think he ever once told me that I was going to need some kind of career to fall back on if or when my plans did not manifest.

For the record, I did become a professional magician but discovered that wasn't going to keep the lights on. Although I'm not a celebrated poet, I'm the author of a dozen or so books. I just would have never guessed that I would be writing self-help books. I still keep that a secret from my twenty-year-old English-major self, and if you're ever time-traveling and meet him, please don't say anything.

None of that is what I'm here to talk about, though. I want to tell you a story about my father and me, about one particular visit when we both knew he didn't have long to live. At the time, I had been a practicing psychotherapist for several years, had published my first book, and was spending considerable time facilitating self-compassion workshops around the country. Yes, you heard me right: self-compassion. One of the upsides to having recognized my constant self-condemnation was that I found my way into recovery from alcoholism and the wreckage of terrible self-esteem that I discovered beneath the addiction.

I received a phone call from one of my brothers saying Dad had taken a turn for the worse and was hospitalized in Oklahoma City where he and my mother lived. I had just finished a three-day retreat weekend with twenty-something participants in Philadelphia and decided to fly directly to Oklahoma to be with my father. Immediately, I was aware of the sharp emotional contrast existing simultaneously in me: the high of being with a group of people learning to reject self-sabotaging beliefs by embracing and being embraced by the compassion all of us deserve, and the deep sadness about my father slipping away. What I could not know at the time was that there was one more very important part of the weekend retreat that was just for my dad and me.

I had seen my father cry one time, on the day his father died. But now, as he and I sat alone in his hospital room, he teared up frequently. I don't know if he was afraid of dying, but I do know that he was convinced that his entire life had been one failure after another. I could feel the shame my dad had experienced in his 76 years gathering in this one small room. I could have sworn it was difficult to breathe.

For the first time in my life, I just spoke directly from my heart to my dad. I told him about what I had discovered in my alcoholism recovery and in therapy. I told him how I'd discovered that even with his best efforts to shield me from that horrible shame he lived in, that shame had still found its way into me. I quickly added that that was not a bad thing, because his genuine wish for me to be proud of myself was there, too.

"Dad, you never even knew you had a choice," I said. "You were treated horribly from the very beginning of your life, and the one person who you knew loved you—your mother—died when you were only eleven years old. I'm so so sorry you had to live your entire life thinking of yourself as a horrible failure. You are not a failure. You are a good man." I have no idea how long we talked that evening, but we spoke of a lot of things, some very serious and sad, some that were just memories we shared, and some of what we said was hilarious. We laughed. Somewhere in there, the heavy shame that had made it hard to breathe was gone, making it easier to cry and laugh.

I cannot know what was most important to my Dad that evening. I hope he felt even a fraction of what I felt at one specific point in the conversation. I know what I said exactly because I wrote it down shortly after I left my dad that evening:

Imagine that your life and my life are directly connected, like a relay. Our life began in 1916 when you were born, and our life will end when I die. Sadly, much of our life was very difficult. There were good times and bad. I know, because you told me many stories of good times. But still, your shame and your belief that you never measured up persisted. Somewhere in time when you handed off the relay baton to me, my part of our life came into being. With that, much of the shame and the self-condemnation remained with me. You added something— something that had never been there for you. You added a message to me that said, "Be proud of yourself, do what you love, enjoy your life." You wished for me what you never had a chance to have for yourself and that wish created a disturbance. That wish made it impossible for me to simply continue our life as it had been to that point. That wish stirred shit up. That wish eventually landed me in therapy and later even landed me in a career of helping people who hate themselves. When we think of our two lives as just one life, we have grown from having no foundation for self-esteem all the way to being a person who helps others out of the darkness of shame. I want you to know that I am a good man because you are a good man. I learned that from you because that was always the truth, whether or not you recognized it. I am also a man with self-compassion. We are men with self-compassion because of the message you added and because of the work I have done with that message. If our lives are one, so far so good. This is a very successful life. I wish you could experience with me what it is like to feel good about yourself and to feel good about helping others move toward love for themselves. I guess the best we can do is that you believe me when I tell you it's a wonderful feeling and know that I accept full responsibility for enjoying my life enough for the both of us. We have come a long way since that day in the hospital, and I plan to keep us moving until whenever my stretch of the relay ends.

We both cried.

Rev. Kathryn Sprague

Rev. Kathryn Sprague's adventures as a pastor began in 1999 after formal Bible college training, ordination, and seventeen years of international mission trips. Since that day, she has served in two churches as a Director of Adult Pastoral Care and guest speaker for Christian groups nationally and internationally. Kathy and her husband live in Fort Myers, FL. Contact her at kathysprague@gmail.com.

Humble Yourself and Pray

ℛev. Kathryn Sprague

I t was at the beginning of my pastoral ventures when a wonderful experience occurred through Scriptures found in 2 Chronicles, Chapter 7. This Chapter tells of the building and dedication of Israel's Temple, kings, wars, and civil strife. God answers a sincere prayer of Solomon's in a dramatic way, with fire from Heaven that consumes the burnt sacrifice the priest is offering. The glory of the Lord fills the Temple like a cloud and the priests of the Lord cannot enter the house of God. His glorious presence had filled it to full measure (vs. 1–2). Now, that's a great day at Church!

All the children of Israel saw this fire firsthand. The people responded by bowing their bodies, placing their faces upon the pavement, and began worshipping God by crying out, "He is good and His mercies endure forever." This was so exhilarating that both Solomon and the people began giving extravagant financial offerings, sacrificing burnt offerings, and praising the Lord in a festival of dedication for twenty-three days.

God's response to a leader who built and dedicated his work to God was when fresh revelation begins to unfold. God appears to Solomon alone that night and teaches him the "If" lesson. It's a lesson we must learn if we want God to move on our behalf.

Verse 14: "If my people, which are called by my name, will humble themselves and pray, and seek my face, and turn from their wicked ways; then I will hear from heaven, and will forgive their sin, and will heal their land." Each phrase of this Scripture is significant. One phrase changed my spiritual life forever.

In 2002, my husband Randall and I were invited to minister in Council Bluffs, IA. Senior Pastor Lonnie Parton of Victory Fellowship Church felt led by the Holy Spirit to conduct a twenty-one-day program called "The Divine Experiment." We were instructed to "fast" all normal entertainment such as TV, movies, video games, and so on. Families were to spend time together doing loving actions such as picnics, board games, talking together, singing . . . anything that was a face-to-face interaction between all family members. Yet, the key focus for each person was the 2 Chronicles 7:14 prayers.

Amazingly, Victory Church watched God begin to do extraordinary things. Family relationships were healed, prodigal children returned home, and a man who walked with two canes was even healed. I was fortunate to be the scribe that penned all the miracles the Lord performed in that three-week period. I began my twenty-one-day journey, and as I began to meditate on the familiar Scripture I would speak the first phrase . . . and then be arrested to go no further. "If my people, who are called by my name will humble themselves and pray" . . . I was mesmerized. The Lord began ministering to my inner self as I would breathe this phrase in prayer. He revealed to my spirit that the current level of humility at which I was praying could only bring a low level of prayer effectiveness.

God is such a loving Father. When He chastens or gives you correction, He does not leave you sad or frustrated, but is willing to immediately give you the answer to your dilemma if you will simply listen. The precious Holy Spirit began teaching me that it was not the "form" of prayer that was getting His attention, but it was a "core attitude level within me" that would affect my prayer's yield. If I would lower body, soul, and spirit, and pray out of that lowliness, God would hear and answer.

Each one of us has dregs of religious pride, unforgiveness, ego, hormonal aggression. For twenty-one days I forcefully meditated that first phrase of 2 Chronicles 7:14, repenting day and night of anything and everything the Lord brought to mind that would keep me from the "lower position." The Spirit lovingly said, "No Kathy, go lower." This quest was a driving passion to see how low I could go.

Anticipation filled me. I knew there would be gold at the end of the trail. I gave God my time for three weeks. I seriously sought the Holy Spirit's help every day for at least an hour, asking Him to help me humble myself to the level that He could effectively move upon my prayers. After three weeks of fasting and praying this phrase of 2 Chronicles 7:14, I was roused out of my sleep early one morning. I felt a shaft of light move through me, unlike anything I've experienced before. I sensed a crystal sword enter my spirit, soul, and body, moving and undulating to its holy presence. The presence of the light was so clean and pure that I vibrated with its glorious attributes. I could only imagine what praying out of this atmosphere would yield. I knew it would change my life and those around me. I was in its vortex and I oozed life, overwhelmed in the loving Presence of God. I loved absolutely everyone and prayer was like a river of gold. In that wonderful experience, God taught me the lesson of humility. The Holy Spirit revealed the "Light of Christ" when I humbled myself and prayed.

Today I am asking you to pick up the gauntlet by setting your heart to pray 2 Chronicles 7:14 as you have never done before. True revelation will always bring demonstration. Go get yours! What do you need from God today? What could His presence do in your family, your church, community, and nation today? Join me. . . . humble yourself and pray.

Robin De Wind

Robin De Wind spent her first career as a respected broadcast journalist covering local news for more than twenty-five years in Rochester, NY. Currently she is the owner of Robin De Wind Media Group, using her unique talent for storytelling to create compelling content for clients, in written and video formats, for website and social media distribution. Born, raised, and educated in Rochester, Robin's unique local perspective and insight helps business owners communicate their professional message with the help of video storytelling. She plans to write a book one day when she gets the nerve. She can be reached at robindewind@gmail.com or 585.317.4898.

Sponge Bob

Robin De Wind

I remember the day I lost my job. It wasn't lost, just line-itemed in favor of someone who was half my age and less expensive. I worked in television broadcasting for twenty-five years. The missed weekends, baby showers, weddings, holidays, late nights, early mornings, brutal weather live shots, and ruined high heels were all worth it. It had become stale.

Now I was a 49-year-old single mother who was being encouraged to explore "new opportunities." I thought at my age I didn't need new opportunities. I was supposed to enjoy being "seasoned" like a nice roast, and not have to worry about being forked. Losing a hefty paycheck and a career was hard to take. Having to look my ten-year-old daughter in the eye and tell her I didn't know what was next was worse.

It was June and third grade was wrapping up. I believe in being direct so I just came out and said it. "Sophie, mommy won't be working at the TV station anymore." They're slashing ten percent of their budget each year and middle-aged, over-priced, on-air talent are being cut first. Okay, I didn't say that, but I thought about it. She was confused and sad but then reflective about how this change was going to affect her status at the lunch table. She cried. Even my mom, who had just endured a day of after-school babysitting, cried.

But then it happened. "Mom, you haven't been happy there for a long time. You used to be Sponge Bob and now you're Squidward." I vaguely knew who Sponge Bob was but, by the disapproving look on my mom's face, even she knew my daughter was right. Sponge Bob is that constantly talking yellow square character on Nickelodeon who never shuts up about how great his job is flipping burgers at the Krusty Crab. Squidward is his miserable, unhappy, unenthusiastic co-worker who hates his job. My daughter had nailed it. Children have this incredible perspective. They sit strapped in the back seat most of their young lives listening to us rant, rave, and complain.

I had to look in the mirror every day for my job, but I had never noticed the reflection she had so keenly noticed.

For 527 days I looked for work. My thirty-year career was now buried on the last page of my résumé that had to be uploaded to an online job application, which then required pages of generic questions and a pass code so a faceless talent acquisition specialist could pick mine from the hundreds submitted.

When I would go on interviews (if I was lucky enough to get one), I would be asked "Can you write? Do you understand crisis management?" I *created* crisis management for God's sake! I was a reporter! But none of it mattered. I was rejected by a job market that had passed me by.

I decided to stop. I took a deep breath and chose to dig in and embrace the daily details that had become my life while waiting for my next life to happen. It wasn't easy because I had nowhere to go, except for driving my daughter to and from school every day. Picking her up was the most fascinating. Fifteen minutes before the bell rings, all the moms, dads, grandparents, and babysitters gather for social networking. It's the stay-at-home version of the water cooler. Friendships are formed, deals are sealed, and numbers are exchanged. I used to loath the moms who prioritized carpools and crafts. I wrote checks. I didn't bake, volunteer, or give a crap about their crap. I would chuckle with superiority at how I was getting it all done.

Now I was forced into their world and what I learned shocked me. They say it takes a village. They *are* the village. It really just takes some like-minded women in crossover vans to get it done. I wasn't sure anymore why I didn't like them. Maybe I was envious. My anger was really all about what I wasn't able to do. Career success mattered, but being present requires more work. I was now able to watch my daughter grow up from a front row seat.

The electric bill, mortgage, and car payment were still sitting there. Creditors were not too enthralled with my over-the-rainbow discovery that there is life after a career. There was also a simple truth—I liked to work and I knew I had more left. There is this hidden network out there of other career veterans who know what it's like to be out of work, too. These are the pay-it-forward people who look out for you in the shadows. They've been through the wormhole, transitioned, and understand the road of humility. Referrals, leads, and introductions were my way out. I was eventually able to say out loud that I had made a career choice and I was in business for myself. Holy crap, I said *what?*

"I'm seeking new opportunities" was finally the truth. At long last it occurred to me that if no one was going to give me a job I was going to create my own. I could be Sponge Bob, I could make the choice to be happy. This is not my ending, it's just the beginning.

Christine Conte

Christine Conte did her "Take 2" as a Certified Professional Life and Leadership Coach. A divorce survivor and "thriver," who successfully juggled single parenting and a demanding career, she empowers women who struggle with divorce, parenting, career, and life issues. Christine has had a positive impact on her community's youth volunteering as an inspirational religious education teacher and a business mentor. As a successful business leader, she speaks at international conferences and universities on leadership. Christine's passion is to create positive change in the world. Visit www.ChristineConteCoaching.com or contact her at info@ChristineConteCoaching.com or 315.657.0493.

The Right Words

Christine Conte

It's not what is said to you that can change your life; rather, it's what you say to yourself. I have had those moments—those embarrassing, wish-I-could-take-it-back, awful moments when I've said the wrong thing at the wrong time. But sometimes the words you speak can impact your life for the better.

In 1995 I was pregnant with my second child. It was the darkest period of my life. Many thirty-something expectant mothers experienced joy in their new baby's arrival. I was experiencing the opposite. I became a single mom, not by choice, but by circumstance, nearly overnight. My husband left me for another woman, announcing this at the two-month mark of my pregnancy. He moved out and I was left to carry the ball alone. My full-time job was very mentally demanding. I had our two-year-old daughter being cared for by a stream of babysitters who didn't stick around more than a few months. I had sole responsibility for our home. I was stuck with the 100-pound, unneutered, male Doberman Pinscher that my husband insisted we purchase three years before. My husband's new accommodations didn't allow pets. I had my hands full and I was barely holding it together.

My mind was in twenty places at once every minute of the day: my job, my daughter, reminding myself to eat, no sleep again last night, how could he do this to me, that report is due to my boss tomorrow, my daughter is sick—call the doctor, here come the tears again, grocery shop, sing my daughter to sleep, feed the dog, remember to put gas in the car, explain to my daughter where daddy is— tell her she'll see him Friday, laundry, clean the kitchen, shovel the sidewalk, the babysitter quit—take time off from work until I can find a replacement, remember to take my prenatal vitamin, change the oil in the dog, let the car outside—oh wait—switch that. Life was draining and at times things seemed out of control.

My job, like the steel structure of a high-rise building, was crucial to keeping everything in place. Without it everything would fall apart. However, I wasn't doing so well. It was the only time in my life I can say that I put less than 110 percent into my job. I wasn't even putting in 50 percent. I was preoccupied with what was going on at home. Looking back I sometimes don't know how I did it, but I do know that my daughter was my first priority. The dog, the house, and the job were secondary or less.

One day my boss called me into her office. "Chris," she said, "we need to talk."

I thought, *Oh, God, no, I'm being fired!*

She told me she was aware of my circumstances, but it was impacting my work and she was concerned that I wasn't up for the job. I listened to her concerns. She was right. There was no excuse for my performance regardless of my circumstances. I tried to hold myself together, fighting back the tears. I told myself a dozen things in those few seconds.

"I know I haven't been doing well lately," I said. "I apologize. You know what's going on at home, but that's no excuse. I will do better. Please, I need this job more than I can express."

I paused, took a breath, and out of nowhere the words spilled out. "He can take everything from me, but he can't take my brain. Please give me another chance."

She was silent for a moment. She looked down at her desk, twisted her mouth to one side, and nodded her head. I got the impression she'd heard those words before—perhaps having told herself similar words at some point in her life. My words connected with her.

She looked up at me and simply said, "Okay."

I took a breath and thanked her repeatedly. I was given a second chance. I walked back to my office. I thought about what I'd said to her. Though the words had come out of my mouth I didn't remember having thought of them. They just poured out as if my soul was speaking. They were the perfect words to express at that moment in my life. They were absolute truth. They weren't the words that she needed to hear; they were the words I needed to hear.

He can't take my brain! I thought to myself. He can rob me of my ideal family situation, and possibly even my prior notions of the future, but he can never take away the essential parts of me—in this particular case, my intelligence. My mind had solved so many problems before. This was just another one. It was a doozy, and perhaps the most difficult of my life, but in the end it was just another problem.

That's how I decided to look at things going forward. I had no more time for tears. I started looking at things analytically as I had been academically trained to do. A difficulty, struggle, or hurdle became merely another problem to solve rather than some overwhelming elusive task. I tackled each issue with resolute determination, solved them, and got them off my plate as quickly as possible. I got rid of the things in my life that I no longer needed or weren't helping me. I even had to give away our dog. He was simply too much for me to care for and deserved more attention than I could give. I found a sitter who stayed with us for more than a year, and who was more like a friend than a babysitter. Eventually I was able to give the right amount of attention to the things that mattered most.

My job turned out fine in the end. I had the baby and went on to do good things for the company. My career flourished at my next position with two promotions, culminating in an article published about my work in a highly regarded industry magazine a few years later.

The unyielding struggles of single parenting walked beside me for eighteen years. My daughters are now in their twenties and are both successful, talented, young women of whom I couldn't be prouder. When I look back over the "eighteen-year blur," as I often call it, I know that I did it all on my own. I'd heard the words I needed to hear most—and they came from within me.

Karen Vosmik

Karen Vosmic retired from commercial real estate where she was a broker/associate for twenty years. Prior to that, she was part owner/operator of a gas station for ten years and learned how to fly an airplane. Currently she golfs, plays cards, travels in a motor coach, is an active member of the Daughters of the American Revolution and also chairs an event for the Naples chapter of Foundation Fighting Blindness. Karen and her husband reside in Naples, FL. They have been married for 56 years and have three children, seven grandchildren, and six great grandchildren.

The Promise

Karen Vosmik

There comes a moment in parents' lives when they think, "I've done a great job! My kids are grown. They're adults with good jobs, families, and homes." It's also at that point when they think they now have the time to kick back, relax, and enjoy watching their children as their lives develop. Until they get the phone call—the phone call that will change their lives forever.

"Mom, I was diagnosed today with stage-four Hodgkin's lymphoma." My daughter couldn't even say the word "cancer."

At that moment, I prayed and cried and then cried and prayed some more. It was time to take action. I pleaded with my daughter to take this to the highest clinical authority for treatment. I took her matter to the highest religious authority, God. Although I've never been described as a devout Catholic, I was willing to bargain with God to save my daughter. As I began my bargaining, I vowed to never miss another Sunday service, and live a life as a God-fearing Christian, if only my daughter's life was to be spared. Bargaining with God was the only power I seem to have and I needed to have some control over this dire situation.

My daughter drove from Chicago to Minnesota to seek advice and treatment from the Mayo Clinic. Her diagnosis was confirmed and the treatment plan began. That was my first prayer answered and I began to fulfill my promise to attend church every week.

Through chemotherapy, biopsies, surgeries, and other clinical treatments, my daughter's battle with cancer was being fought. I was fighting the battle the only way I knew how. One year after she'd begun the fight, doctors confirmed she was in remission. I hadn't missed a week of church. My promise was keeping my daughter alive. I had even started engaging in charity work to further my promise to God.

Fifteen years later, my daughter hasn't had a relapse and remains in full remission, with some doctors calling her *cured*. It was a long stretch from stage-four to cured, and I kept my promise to attend church every Sunday, even during vacations, special events, traveling, and other obligations. It hasn't always been easy, but I've continued my charity work and I try to help others in need.

This experience brought me to my knees and I will not take my promise to God lightly. He delivered. It changed my life and I truly believe it changed my daughter's life, too.

Because of our
unfailing love,
I can enter your
house; I will
worship at your
Temple with the
deepest of awe.

—PSALMS 5:7

Janice Brown

Janice Brown lives in beautiful southwest Florida with her precious Yorky La Duc. She hosts a living room full of ladies for happy hour every Tuesday at 4 P.M. and is an absolute joy to everyone who knows her.

Tips for a Happy Life

Janice Brown

When you think of senior citizens, you may think of walkers, pills, or empty conversations. That's not my idea of a happy life. I'm 94 years young and I feel like my life is picture perfect. That doesn't mean I've never had any troubles because, of course, I've had many, but I choose to live my life full of joy and am grateful for every moment.

As a child, I was on my way home from grade school with my friend, Mary, both of us sliding happily down a snowy hill. I saw my mother motioning to me through a window to come home. When I got inside, mother looked at me and simply said, "Papa died." That was all.

There was an abrupt change in me in that moment. I was nine years old. That kind of shock and loss certainly shapes a child. I was rather quiet growing up, but I was never unhappy. I dreamed of having lots of children and being a loving wife. It was at local dance where I met the love of my life, Ernie Pesola, who would make that dream a reality.

After our first son, Bill, was born, Ernie said one child was enough for him. I smiled but later ended up with five great boys! Our life with our five sons was just what I'd hoped it would be. Ernie and the boys helped me out of my serious nature. They were big teasers and full of fun. We ate together around the dining room table and after dinner we knelt down and said the rosary together. My husband held a yardstick as a reminder that saying the rosary each night was mandatory. We prayed for world peace. I was passionate about my boys and felt I had a wonderful life. But it was not without challenges.

When my son Robert was nineteen, he sat me down to tell me he was gay. I was stunned. I listened to my son pour his heart out, but I didn't really know what to think. At that time, we were the first to have a divorce in the family, the first to have a son who had to get married, and now the first to have a gay son! When he told me, I thought, *Lord give me strength to know how to answer him.* I looked at my beautiful son and said, "Robert, I don't understand. Explain it to me and I'll try to understand." I thought how sad it was for him to have kept this secret for so many years. Keeping a secret is always harder than revealing the truth.

At sixty-four my husband Ernie suffered a fatal heart attack. I realized there was nothing I could do about it and quickly learned acceptance. I asked God for strength and was grateful to receive it when I again faced insufferable heartbreak. My son, Robert, also lost his life to heart disease. He was only forty-three. Less than twenty years later I lost another son, Billy, to the same disease.

I can't think about it. I might lose my mind if I allowed myself. It's got to be God's strength that gets me through. I can't do this on my own. Having a great family and good friends is a big help. Someone I knew who also experienced great loss never got over it. That tells me she had no faith, so no strength. I've never thought *Why me?* Instead, I think *Why not me?*

After the loss of my husband, finding a man was the last thing on my mind. But at sixty-two I met my second husband Bill Brown at our high school reunion. I lost Bill to heart disease at the age of seventy.

We often have no idea how strong we are until life puts us in a position that brings that strength forward. I lost my father, two sons, and two husbands. That's an exceptional amount of loss in one life. So what is the secret to being happy in the face of such great loss? Realizing that bad things happen to all of us; how we respond to them defines our character and our quality of life. We can choose to sit in perpetual sadness or embrace the life we have and rise above.

I never hold a grudge. I still drive myself to Mass every Sunday and every day during Lent. I play a lot of cards, especially duplicate bridge and poker, I swim, walk, and say the rosary every day. I read trashy novels, look forward to happy hour with my friends, and love my afternoon soap operas. Regular exercise is a good part of making me feel well. I treasure my little dog, LaDuc, and can't remember ever not having a dog.

Happiness is a choice. We can either feel sorry for ourselves for things that haven't turned out the way planned or we can adjust to what life hands us and be grateful for every good thing. I wake up every day and make a choice to smile and be grateful.

My tips for happy life
Have a strong faith
Stay physically active
Be socially active
Love a dog
If you want a martini—have one!

Laura Stanley

Laura Stanley and her husband live in Seattle, where she gets to be a stay-at-home mom to their sons August (age three) and Gideon (age one). They have one daughter in Heaven, Penelope, who would have turned five last Thanksgiving. You can contact Laura at laura@willardstanley.com or 561.779.3902.

My Choice

Laura Stanley

A friend of mine posted an article on Facebook sometime in 2013. It was originally printed in *The New York Times*. It's about a woman who found out she was having twins, one daughter who was healthy, and one son who had a life-threatening genetic defect. She chose to abort her son, out of fear for the quality of life he could never have.

After reading the article, I felt sad. What a terrible thing to happen to a woman! I know. I felt I had to share the other side of the story. My side. My choice. I felt like I had to defend my choice for my daughter. My choice to let her live out all of her days. Both of those days.

Just like the mom in the Facebook post, we were worried, terrified, and distraught when we found out our baby wasn't as perfectly formed as we had hoped. I know the thoughts that crossed that other woman's mind: I'll do anything to protect this child. How can I raise someone like this? Why us? What are our options? How will this affect my other children, present and future? We were given many of the same options that she was. We were both looking for guidance. The difference between us is our reaction when abortion was placed on the table.

Here's where I want to be clear: I am by no means saying that I am better for making the choice I made. I'm not saying she was a terrible person for what she did. I'm not saying she is a bad mother. I am saying she needs the hope of the gospel.

Hope is what she lacked for her unborn baby. She knew that if both of her twins survived birth, her new son would need oxygen and life support. His organs were pushed up past his diaphragm into his chest, not leaving enough room for his lungs to develop. She worried, as I did for my girl, about her baby's quality of life. How long could they live like that? What kind of pain would they be in? How would they learn? How would other children and adults treat them, and us as their parents? It's terrifying and heart-wrenching.

She chose to end her child's life rather than have him face that kind of life. When abortion was suggested to me (more than once by more than one doctor) I shoved it aside. I do believe abortion is murder, so that was my initial reason, but it's not the only one. I chose to not end my daughter's life because her life belonged to God.

God created my child, the same way he created the author's. If a child lives for an hour, a day, five years, or a hundred, the date of that child's death is still in God's plan and who am I to negate from that number?

My daughter was born on an early November morning in 2012, weighing two pounds, and only lived for two days, but we used those two days to love her and show her Christ's love. Yes, those days were painful; yes, we miss her terribly and, yes, she struggled to live those two days. But God used those days and the months previous to literally touch hundreds of lives. We were candid about what we went through, and so were our family and friends who shared our baby girl's story.

I could face that awful time because of the hope I had in God. Her Father is in Heaven, ready for her in His time. Christ died on a cross for her sins, inherited or otherwise (I have no delusions that someone who lived only two days didn't have time to sin). The Holy Spirit interceded to teach her the love God has for her, because although her eyes and ears were not whole, her soul is. I have faith that she is with the Lord now, and no longer suffering. I made a different choice and I wouldn't have changed it for the world.

Again, I'm not writing this to condemn anyone. I am writing to share my feelings. She wrote her article as a defense for keeping abortion legal into the second and even third trimester. I am writing in hope that other mothers who face the same decision that she and I faced will trust that their child's life is not in their own hands. I am writing to let others know that abortion is not the only option for a child with birth defects or a frightening diagnosis. Pray for hope, pray for trust, pray for faith, pray for healing. God doesn't regret even one baby being born.

Be strong and take heart, all you who hope in the Lord.

—PSALMS 31:24

Pam Stanley

Pam Stanley loves Jesus and loves sharing Him and His Word with others through various women's retreats and speaking engagements. Mentoring women is her passion. She is an area director to four Community Bible Study classes in South Florida as well as the Director of Women's Ministries at her church. Pam enjoys anything to do with creativity, including painting Christmas ornaments, painting on canvas, doing stained glass, and cooking. She enjoys living in Fort Myers, FL, with her husband Bruce of thirty-four years, has three grown children, seven grandsons, and one granddaughter, Penelope Rose, in heaven.

The Trust Box

Pam Stanley

You hem me in—behind and before;
you have laid your hand upon me.
PSALMS 139:5

The news was heartbreaking. The doctor had told our son, Charlie, and his beautiful wife Laura that their first unborn child, a girl, had zero chance of making it to birth. Charlie said, "We want to name her, Mom, so that when we get to heaven and we call her name she'll turn her head." And so she was named Penelope Rose Stanley.

Chromosome 21 was missing, or maybe parts of it were attached to other chromosomes. They would know more in a week. Charlie explained, "If it's completely missing, it's a fluke, and there can be healthy children in the future, but it's fatal for Penny Rose. If there's parts of it still there, then that means it could be a genetic issue from one of her parents."

Oh, but wait, how do I pray, Lord? If I pray that it be a fluke so that there could be healthy children in the future, then Penny dies! Lord, I don't want Penny to die, but I want Charlie and Laura to be able to have healthy children in the future. How do I pray? Lord, I don't want my children to have to deal with a severely handicapped child. How do I pray? Do I pray that she lives or that You have mercy on my children and take Penny home now? Do I pray that Your will be done? Do I pray that she lives no matter what? Search me and know my heart.

I don't want my children to have to walk through this very unknown future. Who am I kidding? I don't want to walk through this very unknown future. If I look to the left, the outcome is not good. If I look to the right, the outcome is not good. If I look in any direction . . . it's not good. How do I pray?

I'm completely hemmed in. Psalm 139:5 comes rushing into my mind: "You hem me in—behind and before; you have laid your hand upon me." I'm picturing a box and I'm inside, walled off with no good answers in any direction about my little granddaughter. I realize that the only place to look is up. Up to my Father, the God of the universe who knows all, who loves me, and who loves my children even more than I do. Inside this box is the only place of perfect peace because this is my trust box. I can only trust God in this situation. He has me right where I need to be and right where He wants me, trusting only in Him. He knows the outcome and the plan, and every time my racing mind jumps out of the box with its what-ifs and fears, I'm having to mentally rein myself back into the box of trust. I can only move forward as long as I stay in the box! Rest in Him, Pam. He knows. Get back in that trust box.

My very wise pastor said something at the time that has stuck with me: "A short life is not a wasted life." It was profound and perhaps prophetic. Then we saw a movie—*The Odd Life of Timothy Green*—that was very emotional for me. To my mind, the message was "a short life is not a wasted life." Timothy Green was only on this earth a very short time but he had a very profound effect on all those around him and his community. It made me think of Penelope Rose. She, even though not yet born, has had a profound effect on those around her. Especially me. I love her already, and I will love her into eternity. She has deepened my faith in my Father, teaching me to trust. She has scores of people in our church, in Community Bible Study, and in our family, praying for a miracle.

People in church would ask me, "Do we have our miracle yet?" She has her grandfather saying, "The blessing of watching how our son and his wife have handled this news is enough blessing to last me the rest of my life." Her Aunt Julie has comforted me with words of wisdom when I was feeling low, saying, "Mom, thousands of handicapped children are born into just regular families with regular parents and they do well. Just look what Penny Rose will be born into!" She has her Uncle McLaren saying "if there's any couple in the world that can handle this it's Laura and Charlie" We have all been profoundly affected by her little life already.

Charlie and Laura were given all of the options. Abortion was one. They could "take care of this." After an amniocentesis for the sake of future pregnancies, the diagnosis was pseudoisodicentric chromosome 21 with a mosaic monosomy 21. In layman's terms that means that one of Penny's 21st chromosomes had broken up and attached itself to the other chromosomes. They could not know the degree of abnormality until she was born, but of course they didn't expect her to make it to birth. It was such a rare diagnosis that the genetics counselor had never seen this before and couldn't find any research on it. Probably because most couples who hear that kind of diagnosis choose to abort. Our children chose a different direction.

One of my friends, when hearing of Penny's diagnosis, suggested I pray that the Lord take her right away! I was stunned by that and told Charlie.

"Well, Mom," he said, "I'm not going to pray like that because I believe every life deserves to live. Now, don't get me wrong, I don't want a handicapped child; after all how's she going to be a computer scientist like me? But it's not about me, Mom." Hearing my 26-year-old son speak with such resolve and maturity was such a blessing and encouragement to me.

I now have more insight into why people want abortions. Although I will go to my grave believing and knowing it's wrong, I now know why people want them: It would be "easier" in the present moment, but oh, the consequences to be lived with.

A few days after the news I talked to Charlie on the phone.

"Charlie, I guess we just pray for God's will."

"No, Mom," Charlie answered. "Pray that she lives. You know, the people in the Old Testament didn't pray for God's will. They prayed what was on their heart, even being angry and asking questions like 'how long oh Lord?,' and so on, so pray your heart, Mom. Pray that she lives. In fact, the only person that prayed for God's will was Jesus and He already knew God's will."

"Charlie," I said, "then why do we always pray for God's will?"

"There's nothing wrong with praying for God's will, but it's kind of how we give God a 'way out' if things don't happen the way we think they should. 'It was God's will.' But the truth is, it's *all* God's will Mom, so pray that she lives. We want to meet her."

Oh my! What a blessing to hear my son say that. To hear the trust, the faith, and the strength in his voice—stunning. Get back in your trust box, Pam.

I found out that Laura had been writing a blog throughout this tough time. She shared the link with me and I was blessed beyond understanding at the heart of this beautiful young woman. In my eyes, there could not be a more perfect mate for our son. Laura is very quiet, so perhaps I never would have known the depth of our daughter-in-law's heart had Penny Rose not come along.

Charlie and Laura's pastor/mentor and his wife came by their house when the news of Penny came to them.

"Andy and Kelly really know how to grieve, Mom," Charlie said. "Our culture doesn't want to grieve. Instead people try to mask it with drugs, denial, or drink, but we as Christians should grieve the most because we groan with creation, and we should rejoice the most because we have the Savior."

As I trusted, prayed, read the Word, and listened, the Lord would fill my mind with words of wisdom coming from all different sources: "My stomach is in knots but my heart is at peace." "Let your faith be bigger than your fear." From a pop song: "They said life wouldn't be easy; I just didn't know it would be this hard." God has an uncanny way of bringing us the right thoughts at just the right time.

Jerry Bridges, in his book *Trusting God*, said this: "God's infinite wisdom, then, is displayed in bringing good out of evil, beauty out of ashes. It is displayed in turning all the forces of evil that rage against His children into good for them. But the good that He brings about is often different from the good we envision." I certainly didn't envision this for my children!

Trust, trust, trust! God knows what He's doing.

One week we're told that Penny Rose can't possibly live through birth. "The heart is too big for her lungs." To which Charlie asked, "Do we make funeral arrangements, Mom?" The next week it's something very different. After Laura had gone to the maternal fetal cardiologist, they were told that the heart problem, thought to be a reversal of the aorta and pulmonary artery, is not there as they suspected but indeed has all its functioning parts. The message left on Charlie and Laura's voicemail was "the heart is *not* incompatible with life." And so goes the roller coaster of emotion for all of us.

Lord, what in the world does all of this mean???

November 8, 2012, and Penny is still alive! What a trooper! Charlie and Laura went to the obstetrician yesterday and were told that there's a reasonable chance that Penny could live!! They are scheduling a C-section on December 11 and, barring any further complications, Penny will be born. Whether she will live or not beyond that no one knows. I'm so grateful that I know the One who does know. Get back in your trust box!

My heart as a mom worries that Charlie and Laura have no idea what they are walking into, but then again, maybe that doesn't matter to them. They just want to love their little girl. Penny now has an issue with the systolic/diastolic ratio of the blood flow in the umbilical cord. If it continues to diminish, they will take her early. Laura will have to go weekly to the maternal fetal specialist to have that monitored. A C-section could happen at any time if this blood flow issue changes.

Laura's blog entries are stunning. She discovered a Scripture verse that jumped off the page recently. Matthew 10:29, 31: "Are not two sparrows sold for a penny? Yet not one of them will fall to the ground apart from the will of your Father. So don't be afraid; you are worth more than many sparrows." I never noticed Penny's name before. Laura, an artist, put that Scripture verse on canvas with an illustration of a beautiful sparrow spreading its wings up in the corner and framed it for Penny's room.

Then there's another stunning moment: A friend came up to me in church and told me that as she was praying she suddenly had a vision in her mind of God's hands holding little Penny Rose. Amazing, this body of Christ!

Thanksgiving rolls around. Laura is not feeling well. Monday morning we get the call that they've been in the hospital all night and they are taking Penny by C-section. Laura has developed HELLP syndrome, which is a very serious form of pre-eclampsia. We jumped in the car and headed to the hospital.

Penny was born on November 26, 2012, at around 10:00 A.M., weighing in at a whopping two pounds, 10 ounces. It was obvious there were many problems, but she was beautiful and she was *alive*!

She lived for two days. After many examinations by various specialists it was decided that Penny's body would not support life. Just before the nurses came in to unhook Penny from her life support, Charlie led us in prayer saying: "Lord, thank You for letting us meet our little girl, but we're going to give her back to You now because we know You'll do a much better job of raising her than we ever could have." There are moments in life where time stops and this was one of them.

Tim Keller, pastor of Redeemer Church in New York City, says: "The stars get brighter in the sky as the night gets darker; so, too, does our joy become more vivid as our trials get harder."

My husband and I, along with Charlie's sister and Laura's parents, had the amazing experience and joy of being in the room when our son sang to his little daughter as she went to heaven. He sang that beautiful old hymn, "Come Thou Fount of Every Blessing," all four verses, with tears in his eyes and his arm around his wife and little girl. I have never felt the presence of the Lord more strongly than I did in that room in the hospital that day. It was as if Jesus were standing there holding His arms open and saying, "Give her to me. I've answered your prayer to meet her and now it's time to take her home."

The blessing of watching our son step up to be the spiritual head of his home, the loving husband to Laura, and the adoring father to his little girl, was one of the greatest blessings I have ever experienced. As I look back on those days, I can tell you with all certainty that God is a God of hope and blessing and the One worthy of our trust.

Charlie and Laura were able to walk this very difficult road because of their profound love and trust in the Lord Jesus Christ, knowing that He is Sovereign, that He will accomplish His purposes, and His purposes are for His Glory and our good. As a result of this deep walk, Charlie was subsequently asked by his pastors to be an elder in their church. The great news of all of this is that the Lord brings beauty out of ashes and restores where the locusts have eaten. It turns out that Charlie and Laura did not have any genetic issues after all. They went on to have two more beautiful healthy baby boys, both born strong and weighing more than nine pounds each. The doctors said that Penny's condition was like a lightning strike that would never happen again.

These are some of the things that I believe God was teaching me as a result of staying in that trust box:

- As Jerry Bridges said, "God doesn't willingly bring affliction or grief to us. He does not delight in causing us to experience pain or heartache. He always has a purpose for the grief He brings or allows to come into our lives."
- He never puts too much adversity into the recipe of our lives.
- His blending of adversity and blessing is always exactly right for us.
- God never wastes pain.

- God knows exactly what He intends for us to become and He knows exactly what circumstances, both good and bad, are necessary to produce that result in our lives. That intention is for us to become more Christ-like.
- We must learn to trust when we don't understand.
- God is doing a work in my children and in me to bring glory to Himself and to make them/me more Christ-like.
- He will accomplish what He intends to do and it will be *His will*.
- Sometimes on a good day my faith can be bigger than my fear.
- Sometimes on a good day my trust can be greater than the trial as long as I stay in that trust box.
- As Oswald Chambers said, "A saint doesn't know the joy of the Lord in spite of the tribulation, but *because of it*."

And I can honestly say, I wouldn't change a thing!

Krista Dunk

Krista Dunk is a woman of faith who loves ideas, a good cup of tea and, unlike in her younger years, is no longer afraid of a challenge. After feeling small and timid into her early thirties, Krista has now been described as having a gentle spirit and a strong word. Krista's adventures include writing two books, owning multiple websites and small businesses, real estate investing, learning sign language, teaching and presenting, worship, and more. She enjoys living in the Pacific Northwest with her husband of twenty-five years and two teenage children. Visit www.kristadunk.com.

Unique and Small

Krista Dunk

I always knew God made me unique. Even as a child, this truth was written on my heart at Sunday school. However, until my early thirties, this uniqueness was hindered.

I lived small. I felt small. Unique and small—that was me. I didn't lack personal potential and giftedness; I never came close to reaching it. I lacked the desire to fully discover it and had no understanding about how to find or express it.

I was a well liked, good student but incredibly timid. My goals looked something like this: avoid confrontation, be sure everyone likes me, work to be perfect in every endeavor, work to keep things secure and unchanging and, most of all, avoid anything that required using my voice. I had a box and staying in it was just fine with me.

Now I see that an area where my future calling would be—expression and my voice—was under attack. I was often angry inside and unable to express my feelings. Literally, the words would not come. It was as if a lid firmly covered over and closed off my ability to express myself. Strangely, as all this was happening inside, from the outside my life was fairly normal and safe. I was a good kid and most things seemed outwardly fine.

After my parents divorced when I was twelve, my teen years were spent away from church. I made some good choices, like keeping my grades up and staying involved in extracurricular activities, and I made some poor choices, such as destructive relationships with boys and compromising my values to fit in. Thankfully, God was in control. At age twenty-one—newly married—I started attending church again and hearing that God has a plan for my life. But what exactly is the plan?

Every so often people challenged my comfort zone. My husband coaxed my true feelings out of me by never taking "Nothing . . ." as an answer from me when he knew something was wrong. My Mother and sister also talked me into singing a trio with them at church—on a microphone—in front of people—God forbid! I did it, but it stressed me out so badly that my knees knocked, voice cracked, and stomach churned. Another time, a worship pastor commented that I needed to be on stage with the team during services. I responded, "Only if I can put a bag on my head!" Staying small and inconspicuous was my safe and undemanding role, or so I thought.

But piece by piece, God started changing my self-image to match His perspective. Even when I would respond, "Who, me?" because of small thinking, He made it clear, "No, not you by yourself, but with Me." Yes, without Him I truly am small. With Him, all things are possible!

He started talking to me about crazy things like singing on the worship team, public speaking, writing books, being a leader, and other petrifying things! Even as my world and opportunities began to brim with promise, deep down my self-confidence still wavered. Waves of anxiety frequently plagued me, causing physical symptoms. Can I really handle these big dreams and assignments He's giving me? Am I qualified for this amount of vision?

During a conference, one of the other speakers talked us through a visualization exercise that went something like this:

Imagine yourself on a beautiful beach. Hear the waves crashing. Feel the ocean breeze and the warm sand between your toes. You turn and look down the beach and see Jesus afar off. He is walking toward you. Your heart leaps and you run to Him. As you reach Him, He opens His arms to embrace you. While in His embrace, He says, "Daughter, what worries do you have in your heart?" As I listened and imagined the scene for myself, I was surprised at my instant answer to His question: "I'm afraid to be big." He lovingly answered, "Just let *me* be big."

God has helped me become aware of my tendency to become anxious about stepping into my calling. Anxiety is not a way of life. Anyone who struggles with it knows it can sneak up at any time. Sometimes it accompanies the need to be in control. But now I know to turn over all my cares, worries, and stress to God. I pinpoint where the anxiety is stemming from and declare my trust in God for that area of my life. He is always faithful to give my heart peace.

As I look back on my journey, my life is remarkably different today. I have a firm understanding of God's calling for me, and stepping out into new places along that calling's path. It feels like standing high atop an overlook, with an expansive territory in full view. Complacency, small living and thinking, and mediocrity are not ruling me anymore. I lived like that for much too long. No one can continue to live forward while engaging old habits and mindsets.

Each of us has a contribution to the world that cannot be duplicated and each of our contributions are precious. Being unstoppable starts with a decision first, then building an enduring strength which comes from understanding what makes you unique and knowing that God is with you.

Priscilla Wilkinson

Priscilla Wilkinson is a speaker, mentor, and consultant. Her passion is to minister to and encourage women to live successful lives by fulfilling their God-given purpose. She is an active member of Crossroads Presbyterian Church in Stone Mountain, GA, where she serves as an Elder, teaches Adult Sunday School, works in the Fellowship Ministry, and is a member of Women at the Crossroads. God gave her a vision to minister to women through Women of Life, a women's ministry dedicated to mentoring, teaching, and training women to fulfill their calling and purpose. Priscilla is married to Elder Ben Wilkinson. They have three children and three grandchildren. Contact her at priscilla@womenoflife.org or visit www.womenoflife.org.

A Simple Gesture

Priscilla Wilkinson

I t was Thursday, March 1, 2012. I was home, depressed, wondering what I had to live for. I lost my way. I felt alone, unloved, lost.

How could anyone possibly understand what I was going through—the loss of my sister, the loss of my job, the struggles in my marriage, the problems with my children? How could anyone know what it felt like to be such a failure—so worthless? I had nothing to offer anyone.

It was in this state of mind I found myself that day, going through emails, hoping some company had responded to my job application. To my surprise I found an email from Nancy. It must be a mistake, I thought, because the subject line was "Club Saturday." Why is she sending me an email about the club meeting on Saturday? Did she forget that I'm no longer a part of the group? I opened it anyway and it truly changed my life.

> Dear Priscilla
>
> I wanted you to know you are always welcome to visit us at Club. We are meeting at my house Saturday. It is just the usual group attending. Even if you just want to come by for lunch. I guarantee we will be praying for you and we want to support you in whatever other ways you let or want us to. We love you, sister!

Even now, thinking back to that day and that email, I cry. I don't know if anyone can understand what it means to be in that kind of deep despair and have someone say they pray for you, they support you, and most importantly, they love you. I was overwhelmed with emotion. In those few sentences, God used Nancy to touch me and show me His love.

The next day I went to the meeting. I cannot put into words the outpouring of love and support I received. Sitting there in the circle, crying and pouring out my heart, and being accepted just as I was—

broken and in need—forever changed me. I knew I would never be the same again. My life turned around that day because Nancy and the others were willing to reach out to me.

Hope. That was what God gave me through these loving people—HOPE! I began to see myself differently—I did have value. I was worthy. The time I spent that day with all of them was the catalyst for my seeking and accepting God's call on my life to start the Women of Life Ministry.

Today I can boldly speak on the love of Christ and how He accepts us right where we are. He loves us in spite of our brokenness, our sinfulness. And the good news is He wants to use us—you and me—to reach out to others and share with them this same hope and love. In John 15:12 He commands us to "Love each other as I have loved you." That day, many years ago, Nancy and the other women of God did just that—they loved me.

It was such a simple gesture.

Hope is a firm assurance regarding things that are unclear and unknown.

—ROMANS 8:24

Tom Proietti

Tom Proietti is a Resident Scholar in Media at St. John Fisher College, Professor of International Media at Cayuga Community College, and Professor at Monroe Community College.

Written in Red

Tom Proietti

I t was a Friday afternoon, a bit after one. The same seat beckoned me in this classroom as in every classroom. Second chair in the second to last row toward the window. Close to the front, but not too close. Leo McGrady was my professor and he came into the room that September day with a stack of papers—a sure sign that our assignments were going to be returned. This was such a big deal—my first college feedback on my work. The first time someone—some higher authority—might assign a grade to my efforts. My heart began to beat faster, so much faster than I ever anticipated. I could hear the beats. They became a small pounding in my left ear. The first time I had ever noticed the pounding as an audible signal. Why my left ear? Still not sure, fifty-five years later.

Professor McGrady was poker-faced. He was always poker-faced. Deadpanned. He stared at his table and his podium as he set down his folder and the papers. He never looked out at us. Not when he came into the room. It was his ritual. His style. He could feel our presence, but he didn't acknowledge it. No need. He was obviously in charge. The chatter in the air died and silence befell us. Silence and attention.

Do papers come back at the beginning of class or at the end? Or maybe in the middle? Leo did the visual class-attendance-with-glances at each of us. We could always anticipate that. Completely nonverbal. How did he know us already? We were only two weeks in, but he knew who we were. How? He was a priest. Did he have a special gift? A mystical power? I still don't know. We had never spoken out loud in class. Not once.

He didn't reference the papers. The *pile* of papers. It went unmentioned, but it screamed for the next forty minutes. The pile had become a presence unto itself.

He was talking—lecturing, as so many called it. He wrote a few words on the blackboard and underlined a few of them. One word was underlined three times. The word was "paradigm." I don't know why it was underlined and I still don't know exactly what it means. I promise to learn how to use it before I die.

Speaking of dying, I was dying inside waiting for that pile to tumble to the floor. I just wanted my paper back—in my hands. I wasn't even sure how papers got handed back. Did he leave them on the desk and then leave the room? Did he hand back the five best and trash the rest? Honestly, I had no idea. I was so totally clueless—and terrified. I took notes on the lecture, but the pile preoccupied me. I couldn't focus on anything but the pile. I drew several doodles of it and stared at them for reference. I hoped the staring might separate the pile. Break it open. Was mine in the middle? On top? On the bottom? Would the placement be a clue to my performance?

Finally, the professor said the papers had been read and graded, but I only heard "graded." He said we should review our errors carefully, but other than that, there was no advice. As he walked around the room handing back the papers, he said nothing. He walked up to each student and set the paper on the desk. Upside down. I kept hearing "Thank you." Nothing else. Sometimes, "Thank you, Fodder." Lots of mumbling—dispassionate, reluctant mumbles—but no sense of terror. In my heart, I was terrified. I didn't really know what grading was. I had really never had a paper returned.

My paper hit the corner of my desk—upside down. My heart and my stomach: both upside down. My world: upside down. I glanced at the paper, hoping my eyes could turn it over and leaf through its pages. No luck. Only fingers could do that. And they did.

Lots of red marks on every page. Arrows and circles and commas in and commas out, I think. Very red against the black carbon of the Smith-Corona manual typewriter ribbon. On the last page of the three-page paper, Professor McGrady wrote the following in red ink: "You have written well, Tom Proietti." My life was changed forever.

Things have a
way of being
richer in the end,
a product made
better, for the
circuitous route we
take to include all
the elements that
are necessary for
a job well done.

—DAVID WHYTE

Robert J. Guerrera

Robert J. Guerrera and his wife Ginger spend summers in Watertown, CT, and winters living in an active golf/tennis community in Fort Myers, FL. They love animals, enjoy live theater, concerts, dancing and, of course, the beautiful beaches of southwest Florida. They ride the rolling hills of Connecticut on their Harley Road King Classic. They have a daughter, Marnie, and a son, Barret, who live in Connecticut, but make sure they visit sunny Florida during the winter months. They cherish their family and friendships they have maintained since grade school.

Words That Inspired

ᖇobert ᖚ. Guerrera

I was born in a traditional Italian-American working-class family. My parents, three older siblings, and I lived in the inner city on the second floor of a multi-family dwelling in the industrial town of Waterbury, CT. At that time it was known as the Brass Center of the World, primarily due to its military support during World War II. Emmy Award–winner Ken Burns directed a PBS documentary of the four cities that were crucial to the war effort and Waterbury was one of them. Like many families, there wasn't much money, but the sheets were clean and the southern Italian cuisine was more than good.

Educated locally, following high school graduation I was fortunate enough to get a four-year apprenticeship with a large manufacturing company. They made brass products for industrial and military use. Back then it was a real advantage to work in the trade, because manufacturing was booming in this large, blue-collar city. This was my first taste of freedom and it shaped my life.

There were so many apprentices that we had our own classroom and Kaynor Technical High School, a state trade school, sent a technical math teacher to us. It was a typical shop environment with plenty of shop language unsuitable for print. I was really into learning and came in early and left late to do so. Some of the others would rib me about being the bosses' pet but it didn't bother me. Most of it was in good fun, but if it wasn't, I could handle any confrontational or intellectual challenge. Always independent, I knew when to walk away from unhealthy situations—even with close friends. It kept me out of real trouble my whole life. I also didn't want to bring shame to my family.

One day my supervisor told me that the general foreman wanted to see me in his office. Mr. Block (seems funny today but we never called him by his first name) was a stern taskmaster and he would say good morning to us but not much more. The toolroom/machine shop where I worked supported the entire manufacturing division. He took the job seriously and he was the head guy. I thought I was in some kind of trouble or maybe a layoff.

My supervisor walked me to the door and left. Nervously, I knocked (or maybe it was my knees) and I was told to come in. The conversation changed my life. He told me to sit down and said "Guerrera (the big boss never called anyone by their first name or used "mister"), you should go to college for engineering." He didn't mix words. He was always concise and right to the point. I always wanted to do more, and worked with some of the engineers on journeyman-level projects. I had a real interest and would devour the progressively more advanced books they gave me. I was always an avid reader and still am today.

"I've been watching you work hard," Mr. Block said, "and your progress has been exceptional."

I can relive the conversation like it was yesterday and that was many years ago. I said I really appreciated his compliments but I couldn't afford the cost. He told me that the company would pay all expenses. This floored me and I asked him to repeat it. He said as long as it was related to my field, and engineering was, they would pay. I was numb with excitement and, at nineteen years old, I knew I had ability, but no one in the work environment ever singled me out, gave me flight, or made me feel special before. I went home and shared the good news with my family. I was inspired to succeed.

I did well in high school on subjects I liked and just enough to pass on the others so there were no scholarships on the table. This new opportunity was a dream come true and I didn't intend to fail. I enrolled in engineering school while completing my toolmaker/machinist apprenticeship and continued for years with other companies who also paid for my continuing education while employed there. I had other mentors who dramatically impacted my life, but Mr. Block was the first.

Two undergraduate engineering degrees and a master's degree from Rensselaer Polytechnic Institute in Troy, NY, later, I worked my way up to vice president of operations of a high-tech automation company in Fairfield County, CT. A toolmaker with a master's degree was rare and it served me well. Little did I know my true vocation was yet to come.

Teaching always held a special place in my heart. While I progressed in engineering, if there was a subject that the company wanted to teach internally and I was qualified, I would volunteer. I loved the classroom environment and the exchange of ideas. I had spent many years on the other side of the desk. My real chance came after I retired in my early fifties. I had done very well financially during my career but the seventy-hour workweeks required to run a company were wearing me out.

I had invested in real estate as a tax write-off during my peak earning years, and eventually acquired enough real estate to support myself. So began my second career in real estate along with management consulting for a few companies. I enjoyed the freedom and it presented the challenges I needed in life. The fruits of commitment and hard work—qualities I learned from my parents—were paying off.

I had never pursued teaching during my career due to financial reasons. My annual bonus was more than a teacher would earn in a year, not to mention base pay, company car, country club membership, and many other perks. I could never explain to my wife that we had to downsize and pull the kids out of college because I wanted to teach.

I was at a wedding, conversing with a friend who was a school principal. He told me he thought I should teach. I was surprised since I never mentioned it. He knew I had extra time and thought it might be something I would enjoy. He had a close friend with a high position in the state technical high-school and college system and offered to arrange a meeting. After we met I decided to obtain my teaching certification. So began my third career, teaching technical high school and eventually college for the next ten years. I cannot express how rewarding it was, and it continues to be on a part-time basis in retirement.

I share my story with each class at Kaynor Tech. Yes, the same school that sent the teacher when I as an apprentice. I convey that I'm not trying to impress them but to *impress* upon them the opportunities they have and should take advantage of. If *I* did it, so could *they*. They realize we share the same common bond of struggle in our lives. All students are smart, just in different ways. My job was to find that area and feed them knowledge. I also ask them why they think I teach and I get some good answers, such as to give back, to share knowledge, to help with the resurgence of manufacturing in our country, and so on. I give them time to think about it and then reveal the reason. I hope to collect social security for a long time and

I want each of them to pay. They laugh loudly and see the humor but, more important, they see that they can be contributing members of society as taxpayers rather than tax receivers.

The Connecticut Technical Schools are among the best in the country. They have received national awards, and other states visit to model their programs. Students are employed at local companies during their junior and senior years in high-paying jobs. They receive the same offer I did regarding payment for college. But the real satisfaction is when students return after graduation to tell me how well they are doing with their lives and that I had been a part of that.

The most meaningful was when a former student came back and told me he was earning more than his father and helping the family. You can imagine the circumstances and impact it has on that family when a twenty-year-old apprentice becomes the primary breadwinner, especially when you realize an apprentice earns much less than a qualified journeyman. It evokes strong emotions even as I write this.

I believe God has a plan for all of us. As I reflect back on my life I can see clearly that God was always there to present opportunities and guide me along my journey. For that I am forever grateful and faithful.

I spend these days between Connecticut and Florida. Most of my life was spent at local schools and companies, but that is only geographically. I have covered much ground in life due to one experience early in life with someone noticing and giving me a chance with the words that inspired.

A good teacher
can inspire
hope, ignite the
imagination, and
instill a love
of learning.

—BRAD HENRY

Vincent Terrell Durham

Vincent Terrell Durham is a playwright, author, and poet. He resides in the Los Angeles area. He's a member of the Dramatist Guild of America, Alliance of Los Angeles Playwrights, and PlayGround-LA. He writes to honor the Johnson family, who were the best story-tellers a little black boy could ever wish to have. Learn more at vtdisme.com.

It's Never Too Late to Be Who You Were Meant to Be

Vincent Terrell Durham

In the summer of 2011 Facebook was my favorite pastime. Who am I fooling? Facebook is still my favorite pastime. But in the summer of 2011, I decided to put Facebook to the test. I had reconnected with a great many high-school friends, but it was all internet-based. No one had bothered to pick up a phone, mail a letter, or attempt to take our reconnections beyond liking or loving our mutual Facebook posts. I decided that an upcoming trip home would be a great opportunity to see if these reconnections were real or just Facebook pleasantries. I sent my old high-school friends—some I hadn't seen in twenty-seven years—an invitation to meet at a local restaurant for wings and beer. Well, the reconnections were real. People showed up and our high school mini-reunion was a great deal of fun. But the evening gave me more than I had expected. One of my old classmates asked me what was I doing out in Los Angeles.

"I'm working in the accounting department for a trade association," I said.

"You were supposed to have been a writer," He replied, then proceeded to recall a day in twelfth grade creative writing class that I couldn't remember to save my life. "I'll never forget Mrs. Davis pointing to you and saying you were the best writer she'd ever had in her class."

I don't remember this event at all, but I was willing to trust my classmate's memory over my own. Then he said it again. "You were supposed to have been a writer."

Those words stuck with me for the rest of my trip back home and for the entire plane ride back to Los Angeles.

One of my favorite quotes by George Eliot has always been "It's never too late to be who you were meant to be." So with this quote and my classmate's twelfth grade creative writing class memory, I sat down to write.

I finished writing my first stage play in March, 2012. I had no idea if it was good or a piece of garbage. My *Playwriting for Dummies* book said I needed to hear the play read out loud. It didn't need to be anything more than my friends each taking a role and reading for the character. This was the only way I would know what I had. Well, I do live in L.A., and most of my friends are actors, so one sunny afternoon ten people squeezed into my tiny living room and started reading.

My buddy Aundre was drafted to read the stage directions. "Draw Me Happy," he began, "A new stage play by Vincent Terrell Durham."

The actors started reading their parts and what I was hearing sure sounded like a play. I was a playwright. Wow! I spent the rest of that year tweaking and adding to the play. As the year came to a close, I felt confident that it was ready for an audience.

I quit my job in the accounting department on January 8, 2013. That same day, I put a deposit on a theater for the first stage reading of "Draw Me Happy." The theatre sat fifty people, and the day of my stage reading more than fifty people showed up. Luckily, we had extra chairs.

When the narrator read "End of play," the audience applauded.

"It's never too late to be who you were meant to be." I was a writer.

Since then, I've written over forty plays with performances from Los Angeles to the Catskills. In 2017 I received my first commission to write a play. It was presented to me from Planet Earth Arts in association with PlayGround-LA. The piece is titled "Polar Bears, Black Boys & A Prairie Fringed Orchid." The play was presented in late 2018 at a theater in San Francisco.

It's remarkable how another person's memory could have such an impact on my life. I'm grateful that he shared it with me. Otherwise, I'd still be working in that accounting department.

I think people who are creative are the luckiest people on earth. I know that there are no shortcuts, but you must keep your faith in something greater than you, and keep doing what you love. Do what you love, and you will find the way to get it out to the world.

—JUDY COLLINS

Shannon Beaulieu

Pastor Shannon K. Beaulieu and her husband Pastor James C. Beaulieu of Eternal Life Covenant Word Ministries in Port Byron, NY, have two fur babies they consider their children: one a male cat named Sampson, and one a beautiful, little-girl, blue-nose pitbull named Cuddles. They have a stepdaughter, Cheryl Ann Beaulieu, who has two children, a little girl nine years old, and a little boy five years old. She attended three years of ministry school at Mission Global School of Ministries with her husband. She is on the leadership team at Day Of Joy, Inc., and a volunteer since 2011. She has been a volunteer of Joyce Meyer ministries in Hershey, PA, since 2010, a volunteer for Feed My Starving Children at The Vineyards Church in Warners, NY, since 2012, and volunteers at her local soup kitchen and food pantry. She loves to crochet gifts for people in need and newborn babies in hospitals. She has a gift from God for baking and cake decorating. Her most favorite time is spent in the Word of God, study, worship, and daily payer.

A Little Girl

Shannon Beaulieu

There was a little girl who had the incorrect mindset about herself. She even began to mistreat herself. She was very overweight and was always referred to as the fat kid, "Hey, Tubby," and other hurtful names. The kids at school would even moo at her like a cow or oink like a pig to make fun of her. She would cry herself to sleep at night. She never told anybody what was happening to her.

Her best friend always stuck up for her and she was so happy to have her in her life. But in the blink of an eye, her best friend was hit by a drunk driver while playing in her yard and killed instantly. This devastated the little girl. One week later she had more heartbreaking news. Her great grandma, who she adored, passed away as well. She began to withdraw and refused to make new friends or get close to anyone. She was afraid of losing them, with more heartache and rejection. She kept to herself, talking very little to her mom. She spent most of her time in her room.

At the age of seven, her mother's younger sister and boyfriend were babysitting her brother. It was getting late. Everyone fell asleep. Her aunt's boyfriend came into her room and molested her. The girl's parents came home as it was happening and her father caught him. It never happened again. The little girl had that ugly, no-good feeling about herself that goes along with things like that. It didn't go away.

She didn't have the best relationship with her dad. They never got along. He was a very angry, bitter person and full of strife mostly. Verbal abuse was more frequent when her mom was at work. He told this little girl that he hated her, that she wasn't his daughter, that he wished she'd never been born, all while hurling whatever he could get his hands on at her. The situation got worse and food became the little girl's security blanket, so the weight gain continued. Food gave her hope that the feelings of self-hatred, rejection, lack of trust, and feeling unloved would disappear. They only got worse. She didn't trust anyone for fear they would only hurt, mistreat, or use her. She became very closed off and depressed, frequently trying to end her own life.

She finally made a new friend going into middle school. This young lady invited her to attend a youth group and youth rally several different times at her church. It was something that she enjoyed going to, even though she didn't understand anything that was going on. She just knew that the atmosphere was peaceful and none of the kids were mean to her or made fun of her weight. They were always loving and welcomed her with hugs and smiles, which was something she wasn't used to, and had never experienced from people her own age.

At age fifteen she was raped by a local fisherman. This brought on more wrong thinking and mindsets about herself and what her body was to be used for. She just wanted to be loved and accepted. The drinking and drugs soon followed, and she hoped one of them would kill her. Then her horrible life would be over. No more pain, rejection, or feeling unloved. But the cycle continued.

She quit school to take care of her mother after she had surgery and needed care to recover. Her plan was to return to school but that didn't happen. She started working, living at home with her parents for what seemed like forever, and was getting along with her mom. But she didn't have a good relationship with her dad at all. She continued to drink excessively, do drugs, and would meet up with various men hoping that he would be the one. You know, the happily-ever-after stuff. Because of the constant fighting at home with her dad, she would work more, longer hours, double shifts. When she wasn't working, drinking and drugs were on her list of things to do. Partying and bars were her best friends. She was still looking for love, acceptance, and peace.

She met one guy and things were good for the first three months. Then came the abuse, control, and threats to kill her and her parents if she left him. He was living with her in her parents' home at the time. The last straw was when he held a butcher's knife to her throat. That's when she finally told her parents. They called the police and, because he had nicked her a little with the knife and the blood evidence was still on it, they hauled his butt away in handcuffs.

By 2000 she decided it was time to get her GED and a good job. Maybe that would help her be more happy. She was now twenty-two years old, and was still in fear for her life from the ex-boyfriend who was now getting out of jail. She decided to move away and start over. Her parents went with her. She got a new, good job right away. Although the job was amazing, her problems were still there on the inside. They followed her. She continued to drink, do drugs, overeat, and do all the other self-destructive things because her mindsets hadn't changed—only her surroundings.

At her job she became friends with the boss lady who was a Christian woman. She would always invite her to church. Knowing the answer to all the things she was dealing with she would find there, but she refused, because she couldn't go to church hung-over and tired. Maybe next time, she would say. The boss lady didn't give up and the girl remembered how much fun she had had with her friend in middle school at her church. She decided to give it a try. It was the best decision she ever made. The name of the little girl who's story you just heard is now Pastor Shannon Beaulieu.

All the pain, rejection, and feeling unloved was gone. God was right there by my side, keeping me alive, carrying me at times, saying, "No, you can't die. I love you too much. I have better plans for your life and they are good plans."

The church I decided to attend was where I really got to know Jesus. It's also where I got to know my husband James. He was a part of God's plan for my life. I met him at a self-defense class he was teaching. He walked right up to me and thumped me in the middle of my forehead to demonstrate a move to the class. I ran into him a few times after that, but it was at church where we connected, and he asked me out. At first he asked me to have lunch with him, but he called me the night before to talk and asked me if he could pick me up for breakfast instead. We ended up spending the entire day together—breakfast, the mall, lunch, pet store, dinner, and a movie.

Now known as Pastor James Beaulieu, he is an amazing teacher of the Gospel. He's the one who helped me fully understand who Jesus really is, what He did for me on the cross at Calvary, and that He loves me abundantly. He's the one the Lord used to bring me to salvation. Jesus, James, and I are best friends and have been married eleven years.

After meeting the Lord and fully surrendering my life to Him, I fully came out of my cocoon. My husband has been delicately chipping away at it for so long. I have learned to trust, forgive, let go, and to fully love again. We have gone through many storms and trials since being married. None are greater than our God. We have that three-cord-strand bond that cannot be broken. We keep Jesus first in our life and that's what makes things work. James and I went from being homeless, living in missions, to going to Ministry school at Mission Global School of Ministries. We received our certifications, licenses, and ordinations. Since March, 2016, we have been pastoring Eternal Life Covenant Word Ministries in Port Byron, NY. One week after graduating, we were given a debt-free building to start the church in that has an apartment for us to live in and another one for income.

I thank the Lord for the many accomplishments and successes in our lives. He has blessed us so abundantly. I have a strong and confident voice in the Lord and in who I am through Him. The Lord has taken this ugly mess and made her into a beautiful, thriving successful woman of God. No longer trapped inside myself trying to die but full of life, broken free of the cocoon forever by His Love, Mercy, and Grace. Hallelujah! Thank You, Jesus!!!!!

Success is not final, failure is not fatal; it is the courage to continue that counts.

—WINSTON CHURCHILL

Nels Ross

Nels Ross is a husband, father, performer, speaker, and "Chief Executive Oddball" of In Jest, Inc. Working solo and with others, he has uplifted audiences throughout the United States, as well as in Australia, Bermuda, Canada, and Mexico. His diverse background includes studying mathematics, education, and theater at the University at Buffalo; touring with a nonprofit circus; training with instructors from Broadway and Cirque du Soleil; teaching workshops on juggling and life skills; and performing and speaking for companies, conferences, schools, ministries, and others. Visit www.injest.com.

Shift Happens

Nels Ross

C oming from a fairly positive guy, know that it's an understate-
ment when I confess that last year was pretty crappy. Without
boring you with details, here are a few highlights:

- A concussion caused me to be hospitalized and to lose work.
- An organization I worked with went bankrupt, owing me many
  thousands of dollars.
- Major upheaval at home, and my poor responses to it, affected
  family life.
- New York State issued a ludicrously large fine for a small mistake
  in my business.
- I struggled with depression and anxiety over past mistakes and
  future prospects.
- My lifelong friend and original business partner, Andrew Barden,
  passed away unexpectedly.

Change is as certain as death and taxes. That's true whether
current circumstances are good or bad. As it is written: "Change is
inevitable . . . except from vending machines." In other words, shift
happens.

Oddly enough, these events, along with a profound encounter
with a relative stranger, brought about a positive shift in my outlook
and deepened my resolve to practice joyful service.

For context, it might be helpful to know that I'm a performer,
speaker, and "Chief Executive Oddball" of In Jest, Inc. My friend,
Andrew, and I cofounded In Jest in 1992 with the simple goal to
entertain and uplift audiences. And he was a primary instigation . . .
I mean . . . inspiration in my life and career.

We first met while still in our mothers' wombs. My mom called
Andrew my "brother from another mother." From an early age, we
started juggling and clowning around together. That's not surprising,

considering both our parents were involved in clown, mime, puppet, and dance ministry.

He was typically the more adventurous one, convincing me to juggle machetes, ride unicycles, tour with a circus, start a company, and try crazier things like wire walking and fire breathing. (Don't worry, my eyebrows have grown back.)

Even after Andrew's journey brought him to the West Coast and on to other pursuits, we worked together when we could. In fact, we had a blast entertaining at a wedding celebration last summer. So it was a shock when he passed away last fall.

After his passing, I was not performing at 100 percent. Even when the audience seemed pleased, things just felt off. At one such event, I told the host about losing the friend who had inspired much of my silliness. She offered condolences, paused, and made a comment which meant the world to me:

"Remember, as you bring joy to others, he lives through you."

It was exactly what I needed to hear, from a person I'd just met that day. I felt joyful tears welling up in my eyes and had to turn away from the audience as they were leaving the venue.

Who has inspired or uplifted you? A friend, relative, coach, or stranger? Someone who showed you compassion, faithfulness, tough love, or a random act of kindness? Know that as you pay it forward, that person lives on through you.

After this encounter, I took time to consider ways in which I might honor my friend and things for which I'm grateful—especially family and faith. These scriptures were particularly encouraging:

[Christ] died for all, that those who live
might no longer live for themselves but for him
who for their sake died and was raised.
2 CORINTHIANS 5:15

May the God of hope fill you with all joy and
peace in believing, so that by the power of the
Holy Spirit you may abound in hope.
ROMANS 15:13

Like other times in my life, I needed to be reminded that Christ died for me and rose again so I might live—not just for myself, but for him and others. I believed anew that joy, peace, and hope were mine to share, even if only a small taste through laughter. I was also reminded of this Buddhist recitation, which I believe reflects the heart of Christ:

> We vow to bring joy to one person in the morning, to ease the pain of one person in the afternoon. We know that the happiness of others is our own happiness, and we vow to practice joy on the path of service.

In case you're wondering, most of the stuff mentioned at the start has not been resolved. However, business has been good and my financial situation turned out better than I imagined.

Encouraged by Jesus's teachings, a relative stranger's thoughtful words, and Andrew's idea of "philanthropic entrepreneurship," I'm currently working on projects and partnerships to commit corporate profits to worthy causes. And I'm learning that there are as many ways to practice joyful service as there are people in the world.

Austin J. Beers

Austin Beers grew up in East Syracuse, NY, and delivered this address at Commencement as Salutatorian of East Syracuse–Minoa High School's Class of 2018. Austin hopes that by encouraging increased empathy in society, many of the domestic and international plights which we currently face can be overcome. A National Merit Finalist and IRS Certified Income Tax Volunteer, Austin has worked hard to ensure the success of himself and his community. Attending Colgate University as an Alumni Memorial Scholar in the undergraduate Class of 2022, Austin plans to major in Mathematical Economics and eventually pursue an MBA or law degree. Ultimately, Austin Beers wants to employ the skills and knowledge he has acquired to improve the fundamental institutions of society and make the world a more concerned, caring, and compassionate place.

Achieving Success Through Empathy

Austin J. Beers

The following is a typed script of the graduation speech delivered by Salutatorian Austin Beers to the Class of 2018 at Commencement at East Syracuse–Minoa High School, June 22, 2018:

Why I am up here speaking today? Is it because I had a GPA which was second highest in the class? That will be meaningless in about ten minutes. Is it because I remained committed to my academic studies these last twelve years and worked hard to achieve my ambitions? That may be part of it. But the real reason why I am up here, blessed with the opportunity to speak to you all today, is because of teachers like Mrs. Mock, counselors like Mr. Clark, relatives like all of my aunts, uncles, cousins, and grandparents here today, parents like Brian and Elizabeth Beers, and peers like all of you sitting out here today. Every one of you who has had any kind of impact on my life deserves to be up here speaking as much, if not more so, than myself today because each of you has been part of my community of support—my source of empathy.

More so than intelligence, ingenuity, creativity, even perseverance, I feel that empathy is the most valuable trait a human can display. As psychologist Alfred Adler defines it, empathy is "seeing with the eyes of another, listening with the ears of another, and feeling with the heart of another."* Without empathy, there would be no community. Without empathy, there would be no humanity.

With the modern political climate more tense than ever before, with foreign relations strained as can be, and with domestic harmony as distant as we have ever seen, it seems that we are beginning to lose our sense of community, our sense of humanity, our sense of empathy. The lens with which we view success and happiness has become distorted; now that we sit here at the threshold of our future, it is our duty to restore it.

We live in a culture which propels us forward at an ever-accelerating pace, encouraging us to compete with one another and hone our skills in order to rise above the rest. Yet what our culture fails to remind us on our march towards progress is that we cannot elevate our society by rising on our own. We must rise with the rest in order to truly progress as a people and a community.

Our distorted understanding of progress is most pronounced at the venue where many of us will arrive in a few short months: college. According to the University of Michigan's Social and Psychology Review, 75 percent of college students have empathy levels lower than that of the average student in 1980—75 percent![†] Merely one-quarter of us possess the same level of compassion, consideration, and companionship as the generations before us.

We see this loss of empathy all too often during the school day: students sensationalizing their own problems while belittling the issues of their peers, people ignoring the struggles and desires of those around them. I myself share the guilt of this tragedy—all too often do I choose to block out the emotions of those around me, focusing too much on my own needs without regard to the needs of the community.

But where I see this problem the most is in our vision of the future—in the way we define success. What is success? Think about that for a minute. How will you measure your achievements after college? Through the prominence of your job? The admiration of your peers? Fame? Glory? Wealth? Are those things success? While you consider that, allow me to tell you a story—a story which began with a man and a woman, and a son who bore their name.

The couple devoted their lives to their son, the mother showing him intense compassion in spite of her private problems, and the father choosing to stay at home in order to ensure the success of his son's upbringing. The family was not wealthy—far from it, in fact. The parents did not have lavish belongings nor a grandiose house. Indeed, the father had sacrificed his illustrious job in order to care for his child in a way the mother could not.

Many chose to look down on this family, admonishing the fact that the mother was not a maternal domestic and that the father was not employed. But what people failed to realize was that this family shared a bond far more valuable than wealth and status, a love which enabled them to raise a child gifted with the privilege to address his peers with a single message. The son's name was Austin James, and the message: success is not a reflection of one's ability to distinguish oneself from the community. Success is the willingness for a person to devote himself to the happiness and well-being of another.

All of the trials and tribulations we have endured, all of the sadness and joy we have experienced on our path towards graduation become meaningless if we do not all support each other to become a single success story. As we commence on our journey toward our future, we must remember not to let our vision become distorted. We must remember to embrace the values of those around us, and accept responsibility for the fate of our peers. We must remember to thank those who exhibit empathy and return such compassion to our community.

We must remember that each and every one of us, whether we seek to enter college or join the military, whether we plan to start a career or take a year off, whether we are innovative or indecisive, whether we are wealthy or poor, whether we are quiet or loud, whether we stand alone or in a crowd, we are all capable of expressing empathy. We are all capable of having a positive impact on another person's life.

That impact, my friends, is how we will define our culture. That impact is how we will define our community. That impact is how we will define our success! Thank you.

Works cited:
*Dee, Kevin. "Eagle Staffing." Eagle Professional Resources Inc., 29 Apr. 2016.
†Zaki, Jamil. "What, Me Care? Young Are Less Empathetic." *Scientific American*, 1 Jan. 2011.

Ten Fundamentals of Happiness

- Develop a warm outgoing personality with a sincere love of people
- Develop an organized, planned lifestyle with little chaos
- Get in the habit of giving more than receiving
- Pursue a productive, exciting, and active life
- Engage in meaningful activities every day
- Avoid needless worry over trifling matters
- Devote time to fun and play
- Learn to live in the present
- Set realistic goals
- Think positively
- Be grateful